SCHOLASTIC
Data Handling

Year 1

IMPORTANT – Permitted use and warnings

Copyright in the software contained in this CD-ROM and in its accompanying material belongs to Scholastic Limited. All rights reserved.

© 2011, Scholastic Ltd.

Save for these purposes, or as expressly authorised in the accompanying materials, the software may not be copied, reproduced, used, sold, licensed, transferred, exchanged, hired, or exported in whole or in part or in any manner or form without the prior written consent of Scholastic Ltd. Any such unauthorised use or activities are prohibited and may give rise to civil liabilities and criminal prosecutions.

The material contained on this CD-ROM may only be used in the context for which it was intended in *Scholastic Data Handling* and is for use only in the school which has purchased the CD-ROM, or by the teacher who has purchased the CD-ROM. Permission to download images is given for purchasers only and not for users from any lending service. Any further use of the material contravenes Scholastic Ltd's copyright and that of other rights holders.

This CD-ROM has been tested for viruses at all stages of its production. However, we recommend that you run virus-checking software on your computer systems at all times. Scholastic Ltd cannot accept any responsibility for any loss, disruption or damage to your data or your computer system that may occur as a result of using either the CD-ROM or the data held on it.

SCHOLASTIC

Book End, Range Road, Witney, Oxfordshire, OX29 OYD
www.scholastic.co.uk

© 2011, Scholastic Ltd

123456789 1234567890

British Library Cataloguing-in-Publication Data
A catalogue record for this book is available from the British Library.

ISBN 978-1407-12519-0
Printed by Bell & Bain
CD duplicated by Media Plant

Text © 2011 Ann Montague-Smith and Julia Stanton

Ann Montague-Smith and Julia Stanton hereby assert their moral right to be identified as the authors of this work in accordance with the Copyright, Designs and Patents Act 1988.

All rights reserved. This book is sold subject to the condition that it shall not, by way of trade or otherwise, be lent, hired out or otherwise circulated without the publisher's prior consent in any form of binding or cover other than that in which it is published and without a similar condition, including this condition, being imposed upon the subsequent purchaser.

No part of this publication may be reproduced, stored in a retrieval system, or transmitted, in any form or by any means, electronic, mechanical, photocopying, recording or otherwise, other than for the purposes described in the lessons in this book, without the prior permission of the publisher. This book remains in copyright, although permission is granted to copy pages where indicated for classroom distribution and use only in the school which has purchased the book, or by the teacher who has purchased the book, and in accordance with the CLA licensing agreement. Photocopying permission is given only for purchasers and not for borrowers of books from any lending service.

Due to the nature of the web we cannot guarantee the content or links of any site mentioned. We strongly recommend that teachers check websites before using them in the classroom.

Authors
Ann Montague-Smith and Julia Stanton

Commissioning Editor
Paul Naish

Development Editors
Kate Pedlar and Pollyanna Poulter

Editor
Niamh O'Carroll

Series Designer
Andrea Lewis

Designer
Ricky Capanni (International Book Management)

Illustrator
International Book Management

Credits & Acknowledgements
© Crown copyright material is reproduced under the terms of the Click Use Licence.

MIX
Paper from responsible sources
FSC® C007785

Contents

Introduction		4
Lesson 1 - Science:	Leaves	6
Lesson 2 - Science:	Sorting again	8
Lesson 3 - Science:	Clothes that keep us dry	10
Lesson 4 - Science:	Fruit	12
Lesson 5 - PSHE:	Fruit and vegetables	14
Lesson 6 - Science:	Chicken and eggs	16
Lesson 7 - Geography:	Holiday travel	18
Lesson 8 - Music:	Musical instruments	20
Lesson 9 - Science:	Melting ice	22
Lesson 10 - English:	Shopping	24
Lesson 11 - PSHE:	My family	26
Lesson 12 - PSHE:	Inside my home	28
Lesson 13 - Science:	The weather	30
Lesson 14 - History:	Children's toys	32
Lesson 15 - PSHE:	Clothes game	34
Lesson 16 - Science:	Growing seeds	36
Lesson 17 - History:	Our parents' toys	38
Lesson 18 - Geography:	Holidays	40
Lesson 19 - Science:	Things that work with electricity	42
Lesson 20 - Science:	Farm animals	44
Lesson 21 - D&T:	Model testing	46
Further ideas		48

Introduction to Scholastic Data Handling

About the series
Scholastic Data Handling is designed to support primary teachers by helping their students in using important data-handling skills every day. Each title in the series provides opportunities for using relevant data within all subject areas, as defined by the National Curriculum. By using the series, a teacher or school can be confident that they are embedding data handling, so that children are given real opportunities to find data from sources such as other people, books and the internet, and to use data in a variety of practical ways.

The importance of data handling
Every day we encounter data. This might be through television programmes, internet searches to find the best price for something, comparing costs in shops, and in discussions with others. Children will come across data from very early on, such as how many grapes each of them in a group has, how tall their tower of bricks is compared with those of others, and so on. As children become older and develop their own interests, they will encounter data in areas such as sports and their results, shopping and getting good value for money, or where they might go on holiday.

In order to foster development in data handling, children need to experience using real data, in real-life situations, as often as possible, so that they make the connections between what they learn at school and life outside school. Eventually, when children leave education and begin employment, data-handling skills will be vital to them in managing their work and living in society.

About this book
This book provides full coverage of the Data Handling strand from the Primary National Strategy: *Framework for Teaching Mathematics*.

Each double-page lesson consists of one page with lesson details and a second, photocopiable, activity sheet typically showing a data-handling diagram, chart or graph. Where possible, data-handling software, such as a graphing or pictogram tool, is incorporated into the lesson. Children's own data can be captured using this software, then displayed on the interactive whiteboard for all to see and discuss.

Across the series, each area of the National Curriculum is visited. If a subject area does not lend itself well to realistic data for a certain age range, this has been left for a later book to ensure the data is always pertinent.

Lesson structure
Each lesson contains:
- Mathematics objective(s) for the relevant year group taken from the Primary National Strategy for Mathematics and the National Curriculum. At least one objective from the data-handling strand is included for every lesson. National Curriculum objectives have been abbreviated, but full details can be found on a planning grid in the 'planning' area of the CD-ROM. Subject-specific objective(s) taken from the National Curriculum requirements or guidelines for the subject are also included.
- The vocabulary that specifically relates to the data handling content of the lesson.
- A list of resources, including practical materials, activity sheets that can be displayed or printed and references to images and interactive data-handling tools on the CD-ROM.

Resources
- Seeds, such as sunflower or runner bean; pots, compost, gardening equipment; uniform non-standard units of length, such as interlocking cubes

CD-ROM slideshow:
- Activity sheets: 'Growing seeds – table' (two copies for each child), 'Growing seeds block graph' (two copies for each child) and 'Sunflower challenge' (also p37)
- Images: 'Growing sunflower'; 'Growing seeds'
- Block graph tool

- An introduction to the lesson, including questions to ask the children about the topic and the data.
- The children's task, which may be for group, paired or individual work.
- Differentiation to help you decide how to help the less confident learners in your group or class, and how to extend the learning for the more confident.
- A review of the lesson, where children's work may be considered, or where further data is introduced. This section includes more questions to ask the children in order to identify their level of understanding.
- A 'Now try this…' section, which has further ideas for activities based on the curriculum topic and its data-handling possibilities.
- CD-ROM follow-up material, which consists of images to stimulate enquiry or use of the data-handling tools to extend the investigation.
- An activity sheet with material which may form part of the Introduction, the Children's task or the Review.

Introduction

How to use the CD-ROM
- The CD-ROM needs to be installed. Double-click the 'installDHYear1.exe' file, and follow the instructions onscreen to install the software to your network or computer. If you or your school has purchased more than one *Scholastic Data Handling* title, these will all feed into the same, single, *Scholastic Data Handling* program.
- The opening menu asks you to choose between a Teacher Zone and a Kids Zone.

Kids Zone
- The Kids Zone comprises eight maths tools to create and print: sorting and Venn diagrams; Carroll diagrams; pictograms; tables and charts; block graphs; bar charts; line graphs and pie charts.

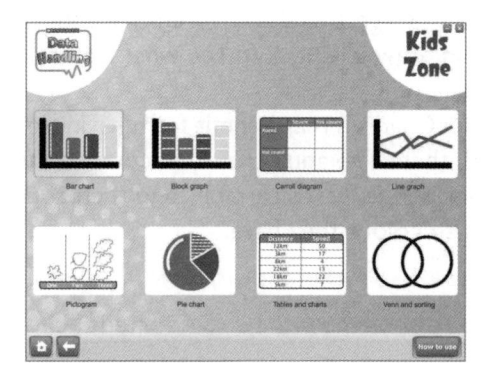

Teacher Zone
- **The Teacher Zone is password-protected. The password is: login.**
- Once in this zone, the relevant year group can be selected, which takes you to a lesson menu. There is at least one ready-made slideshow per lesson that includes all the CD-ROM resources needed: images, activity sheets, ready-made 'interactive' graphs, Word documents and so on. 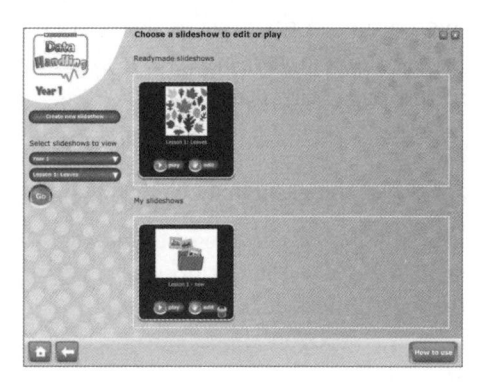
- It is possible to edit or create bespoke slideshows, selecting from all the resources provided for all years that have been installed. It is also possible to upload your own resources into the *Scholastic Data Handling* program. Bespoke slideshows are saved in the 'My slideshows' area.

Slideshow resources across the series include:
- Activity sheets as PDF files that can be printed or displayed, and editable activity sheets in Word or Excel. Images and video which can be displayed on a computer or interactive whiteboard.
- The same tools provided in the Kids Zone, as well as ready-made 'interactives' within slideshows.

A more detailed 'How to use' document is provided on the CD-ROM.

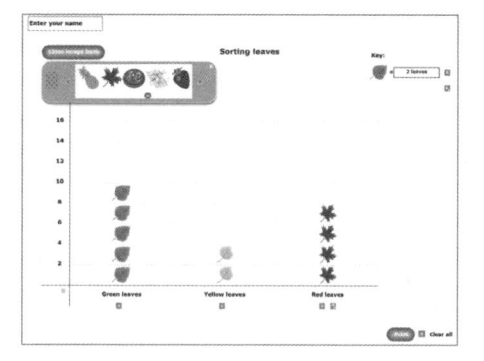

How to integrate data handling within a cross-curricular approach
When data handling is used as part of a topic or investigation, it gives children some insights into how they can use what they know in different curriculum areas, and in real life. The data handling in this series of books evolves naturally from the topics. In this way the children will experience data that is realistic, and relevant to them. Similarly, the 'Now try this...' section of the lessons gives further examples of collecting and using data in real-life situations. Within any topic there will be specific aspects of handling data that fit well within the subject matter. It is much better to use those aspects of handling data where they arise naturally, rather than try to 'force' data from topics.

This book provides opportunities for children to collect data, then organise it. There are opportunities to make tables, diagrams and graphs, as appropriate to the topic. There are also lots of opportunities to ask questions about the data, and to compare the class or individual children's data with that contained in the tables or graphs on the photocopiable pages provided in the book and on the CD-ROM.

Leaves

Lesson 1

Mathematics learning objectives
Framework:
- **U&A:** Answer a question by selecting and using suitable equipment, and sorting information, shapes or objects; display results using tables and pictures.
- **HD:** Answer a question by recording information in lists and tables; present outcomes using practical resources, pictures, block graphs or pictograms.

NC: Ma2, 1g ; Ma2, 5a

Science learning objectives (NC)
- **Sc1, 2f:** Explore, using the senses of sight, hearing, smell, touch and taste as appropriate, and make and record observations and measurements.
- **Sc1, 2g:** Communicate what happened in a variety of ways, including using ICT (for example, in speech and writing, by drawings, tables, block graphs and pictograms).

Vocabulary
Colour names, pictogram, sort

Resources
- Real leaves from trees and shrubs, (smaller leaves will be easier to stick onto the pictogram sheet), sorting rings and glue sticks

CD-ROM slideshow:
- Activity sheets: 'Pictogram' (enlarged to A2) and 'Sorted leaves' (also p7)
- Images: 'Autumn leaves', 'Flowers', 'Spring leaves' and 'Mixed leaves'
- Pictogram tool

Introduction
Look at the image 'Autumn leaves' from the CD-ROM. Talk about what the children see: the leaves are different colours, shapes and sizes. Provide each group with some leaves collected earlier, or, if time allows, take the children outside to collect their own. Explain to the children that you would like them to look closely at the leaves. Ask questions such as:
- *What colours can you see?*
- *Do you think all the greens are the same?*
- *What other colours can you see?*
- *Now what about shape. Are all the leaves the same shape? Tell me what you can see.*

Discuss the structure of the leaves: the veins, the stalks. Encourage the children to look carefully at the leaves.

Children's task
Working in small groups, with leaves, sorting rings and the activity sheet 'Pictogram' from the CD-ROM, ask the children to sort the leaves by colour. They should use the sorting rings to help them and then place their leaves onto the pictogram for you to check. If necessary, remind the children that the leaves should be evenly spread. Ask them to count how many leaves there are for each colour. Now ask the children to repeat this for a different way of sorting that they choose for themselves. They can glue the leaves onto their sheet as a record.

Differentiation
More confident: Suggest to the children that they choose a leaf and draw it. Check to see what features of the leaf they include.

Less confident: Children may benefit from having an adult work with them. The adult should encourage the children to describe the leaves carefully, and then count how many of each colour they have.

Review
Ask each group to show how they have sorted their leaves. Ask:
- *How did you sort your leaves?*
- *How many brown/yellow/spiky leaves were there?*
- *Has everyone sorted in the same way?*
- *How else could we sort these leaves?*

Reveal the pictogram tool. Take one group's work and ask the children to say how many leaves there are in each of their groupings. Using the leaf icons or coloured counter icons to represent each leaf, place these into the pictogram. Discuss how the counters are equally spaced so that it is easy to see how many each column/row has, and which have more or fewer.

Look at the pictogram on the activity sheet 'Sorted leaves'. Ask: *Is this the same as your pictogram?* Discuss the questions on this page with the class.

Now try this...
Children can sort other things such as fruit, vegetables, lunch boxes and flowers.

CD-ROM follow-up material
Display the images 'Flowers', 'Spring leaves' and 'Mixed leaves' from the CD-ROM on the whiteboard. Ask the children in their groups to make a list of the different ways these sets of objects could be sorted.

Lesson 1

Sorted leaves

■ Look at the pictogram below. It shows how some leaves have been sorted.
■ Then answer the questions.

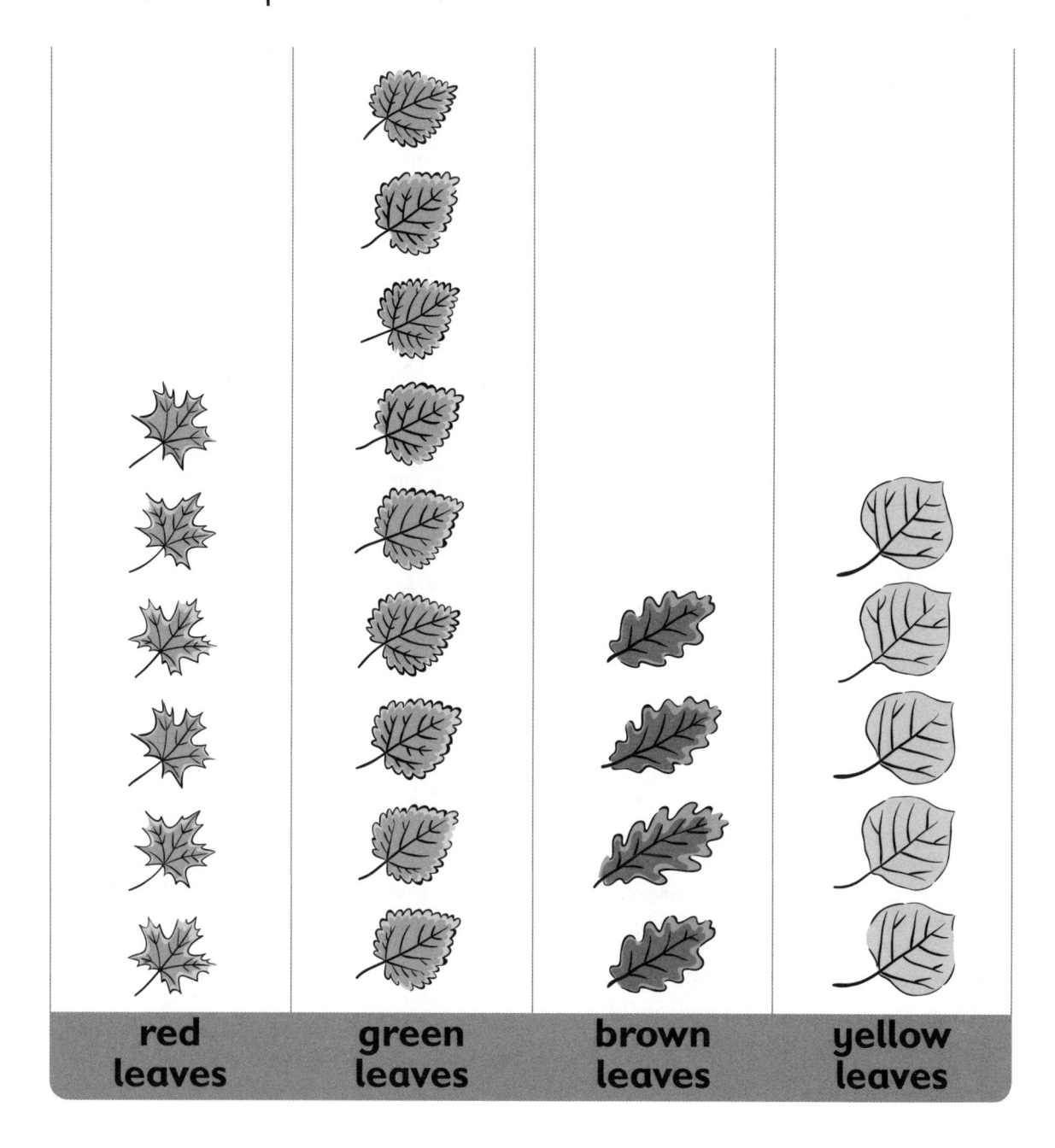

| red leaves | green leaves | brown leaves | yellow leaves |

1. Which colour has the greatest number of leaves? How can you tell?
2. Which colour has the least number of leaves?
3. How many brown and yellow leaves are there altogether?
4. How many more red leaves are there than yellow leaves?
5. How many fewer red leaves are there than green leaves?

Scholastic Data Handling Year 1

Lesson 2

Sorting again

Mathematics learning objective
Framework:
- **HD**: Use diagrams to sort objects into groups according to a given criterion; suggest a different criterion for grouping the same objects.

NC: Ma2, 5a-b

Science learning objectives (NC)
- **Sc1, 2f**: Explore, using the senses of sight, hearing, smell, touch and taste as appropriate; make and record observations and measurements.
- **Sc1, 2g**: Communicate what happened in a variety of ways, including using ICT (for example, in speech and writing, by drawings, tables, block graphs and pictograms).

Vocabulary
Colour names, larger, largest, size, smaller, smallest, sort

Resources
- Real leaves from the previous lesson, sorting rings, glue sticks, a selection of shells for sorting (optional)

CD-ROM slideshow:
- Activity sheets: 'Sorting ring' (enlarged to A3) and 'Shells from Windy Beach' (also p9)
- Images: 'Shells' 1 and 2

Introduction
Review the previous lesson where the children sorted the leaves by colour. Explain that the leaves could be sorted in different ways. Provide each group with some leaves or display the leaf images, from the CD-ROM, from the previous lesson. Ask the children to think of another way to sort the leaves. They might suggest by their size; by their shape; whether or not the edges are jagged or smooth, and so on. Encourage the children to look closely at the leaves in order to help them to consider each suggestion. Demonstrate one way of sorting using the sorting rings. For example, label one ring 'Large leaves' and sort so that all the larger leaves are inside the ring, and the others lie outside it.

Children's task
Ask the children to work in small groups. They can use the sorting rings to decide how to sort their leaves.

Now ask them to think of another way they could sort their leaves and repeat the task. Each group should decide together which way of sorting they prefer, and should stick the leaves onto an A3 enlargement of the activity sheet 'Sorting ring'. Write the label on the page for the children if necessary.

Display the image 'Shells 1' from the CD-ROM and the activity sheet 'Shells from Windy Beach'. Discuss how the shells were sorted in the diagram and answer the questions together. Ask the children if they can think of any other way to sort the shells. If time permits give groups some shells, or images of shells, and ask them to sort them using the sorting rings.

Differentiation
More confident: Encourage the children to think of more ways of sorting. Suggest that they look very closely at the leaves and the shells to spot similarities and differences.

Less confident: Discuss with the children how they could sort their leaves and shells, and ask them to do this into and outside a sorting ring. If they cannot think of another way of sorting, make some suggestions.

Review
Share each group's completed 'Sorting ring' page with the class, covering each label to begin with. Ask:
- *How do you think these leaves have been sorted?*
- *How many are inside the ring?*
- *How many leaves are outside the ring? Why are there leaves outside the ring?*

Reveal the label and invite the children to suggest other ways of sorting their leaves.

Next, ask each group to show you how they sorted their shells. Ask:
- *How were the shells from Windy Beach sorted?*
- *How did you sort your shells?*
- *Can you think of another way to sort the shells?*

Now try this...
Children can sort other collections, such as:
- shape blocks
- toy cars
- fruit
- pictures of fish (cut from magazines).

CD-ROM follow-up material
Display the image 'Shells 2' from the CD-ROM on the whiteboard. Ask the children in their groups to make a list of the different ways the shells could be sorted.

Scholastic Data Handling Year 1

Lesson 2

Shells from Windy Beach

- Look at the sorting ring below. It shows how some shells have been sorted.
- Then answer the questions.

1. How many starfish are there altogether?
2. How many starfish are inside the ring?
3. How many starfish are outside the ring?
4. Do all the shells outside the ring look the same?
5. Name one thing that is different about some of the shells outside the ring.

Scholastic Data Handling Year 1

PHOTOCOPIABLE SCHOLASTIC
www.scholastic.co.uk

Lesson 3

Clothes that keep us dry

Mathematics learning objective
Framework:
- **HD:** Use diagrams to sort objects into groups according to a given criterion; suggest a different criterion for grouping the same objects.

NC: Ma2, 5a-b

Science learning objective (NC)
- **Sc3, 1b:** Sort objects into groups on the basis of simple material properties (for example, roughness, hardness, shininess, ability to float, transparency and whether they are magnetic or non-magnetic).

Vocabulary
Fewer than, how many, more than, sort

Resources
- Basket of indoor and outdoor clothes such as: scarves, coats, macs, hats, shoes, wellington boots, socks, jumpers, trousers, skirts; sorting rings, scissors, glue sticks, shoes or images of shoes (optional)

CD-ROM slideshow:
- Activity sheets: 'Fruit and sweets' (also p11), 'Sorting ring' (enlarged to A3), 'Clothes' and 'Shoes sorted by class 1A'
- Interactive sorting ring: 'Fruit and sweets'

Introduction
Display the activity sheet 'Fruit and sweets'. Discuss with the children how the items have been sorted and what labels should be used inside and outside the sorting rings. Ask the children if they can think of any other ways of sorting the items.

Use the 'Interactive sorting ring' to show the children how different items (fruit, leaves, sweets etc) can be sorted and labelled. Put out two sorting rings, one labelled 'Clothes that keep us dry'. Show the children the basket of clothes. Invite one child to choose an item from the basket. Ask: *Will that keep us dry? How do you know that?* Ask the child to decide whether to put the item into the labelled ring or into the other one. Repeat this for other choices of clothes until most of the clothes have been sorted and there are some in each ring. Now ask:
- *Which clothes keep us dry?*
- *What about these other clothes? How could we label these?*

Invite suggestions from the children for labels. The simplest label is probably 'Clothes that do not keep us dry.'

Children's task
Ask the children to work in pairs with an A3 copy of the activity sheet 'Sorting ring' and the activity sheet 'Clothes'. They cut out the clothes, then sort the pictures onto the 'Sorting ring' so that all the clothes inside the circle are 'Clothes that keep us dry'. Ask them to decide how they would label the clothes outside the sorting ring. Invite them to draw at least one additional item of clothing to place inside the ring and another to place outside the ring, and give them the opportunity to discuss their choices with another pair.

Differentiation
More confident: When they have completed the task introduce two- and three-circle Venn diagrams using the 'Interactive sorting ring'. Ask the children to find another way to sort the clothes.

Less confident: Encourage the children to explain why they have placed clothes inside/outside the circle so that they can demonstrate that they understand that the clothes inside the circle all share one property.

Review
Invite one pair to show the other children their sorting. Ask questions such as:
- *What label do you think we should write for the clothes inside the ring?*
- *What about the clothes outside the ring? What label do these need?*
- *Who has thought of another way of sorting the clothes? What label would you write for this way of sorting?*

Now try this...
Children can try sorting the following items:
- clothes which keep us cool and clothes which do not
- shopping, into sweet and not sweet
- artefacts which make a noise/music and those which do not
- images of hot places and cold places.

CD-ROM follow-up material
Give each pair a copy of the activity sheet 'Shoes sorted by Class 1A' and ask them to work together to answer the questions. Discuss answers as a class before selecting pairs to tell you if they would have sorted the shoes differently. If time permits, give children shoes or images of shoes and ask them to do their own sorting.

Lesson 3

Fruit and sweets

- Look at the sorting ring below. It shows how some fruit and sweets have been sorted.
- Write labels for these in the boxes inside and outside the ring.
- Then answer the questions.

1. How have these fruit and sweets been sorted?
2. Have they been sorted correctly?
3. How else could we sort the fruit and sweets?

Fruit

Lesson 4

Mathematics learning objectives
Framework:
- **U&A:** Answer a question by selecting and using suitable equipment, and sorting information, shapes or objects; display results using tables and pictures.
- **U&A:** Describe ways of solving puzzles and problems, explaining choices and decisions orally or using pictures.
- **HD:** Use diagrams to sort objects into groups according to a given criterion; suggest a different criterion for grouping the same objects.

NC: Ma2, 1a-c; Ma2, 1g; Ma2, 5a-b

Science learning objectives (NC)
- **Sc1: 2f:** Explore, using the senses of sight, hearing, smell, touch and taste as appropriate; make and record observations and measurements.
- **Sc1: 2g:** Communicate what happened in a variety of ways, including using ICT (for example, in speech and writing, by drawings, tables, block graphs and pictograms).

Vocabulary
Count, group, set, sort

Resources
- Safety scissors, glue stick, selection of fruit

CD-ROM slideshow:
- Activity sheets: 'Sorting ring' (one A2 copy and one A3 copy for each pair of children), 'Fruit', 'Sorting fruit – A' (also p13) and 'Sorting fruit – B'
- Images: 'Fruit' 1–10

Introduction
Display the fruit images from the CD-ROM and name all the pieces of fruit together. Invite ten children to the front of the class to each 'become' a fruit, each holding a picture or piece of fruit. Ask the children to help you to sort the fruit. Ask: *Which kinds of fruit are usually red?* Invite responses and ask those whose fruit is red to place themselves onto the A2 copy of 'Sorting ring'. Discuss where the other fruit should fit and why (outside the circle because these are not red). Ask questions such as:

- *Which kinds of fruit are red/not red?*
- *Can you think of another fruit that is red?*

Children's task
Ask the children to work in pairs with the activity sheet 'Fruit' and an A3 copy of 'Sorting ring'. They need to cut out the pictures. Remind the children to do this quickly but neatly. Challenge the children to take turns to think of a way in which the fruit pictures can be sorted. Ask them to choose at least two different ways of sorting and check that they have placed all the pieces of fruit in the correct place. For example, they could sort by shape, size, has 'skin' that can be eaten, and so on. Each pair should decide on their favourite way of sorting and glue the pictures in the correct place on the activity sheet.

Differentiation
More confident: Challenge the children to think of more ways to sort the pictures. They can share these ideas later in the lesson review.

Less confident: Provide a suggestion for sorting so that they can begin the activity. Ask the children to describe what they can see and what they know about each fruit, so that they can think about specific criteria.

Review
Invite pairs to show their sorting to the rest of the class. Ask:
- *How do you think this was sorted?*
- *How did you work that out?*
- *How many pieces of fruit are inside/outside the circle?*
- *What label should we give this sorting?*

Ask the more confident learners if they have any other ideas for sorting. Discuss how one set of things can often be sorted, and then sorted again in a different way. Ask:
- *Which way of sorting would you choose?*
- *Why do you like that way best?*

Now try this...
The children could try sorting the following items in similar ways:
- natural materials
- classroom items.

CD-ROM follow-up material
Give the activity sheets 'Sorting fruit – A' and 'Sorting fruit – B' to different groups of children. Ask them to discuss the diagram and answer the questions. Bring the class back together and discuss the difference between the sorting by the two classes. (All the fruit sorted by 1A can be eaten without peeling first.)

Lesson 4

Sorting fruit – A

- This sorting diagram shows fruit that has been sorted by Class 1A.
- Look at the diagram and then answer the questions.

1. How do you think the children have sorted the fruit?
2. What other fruit could fit in this sorting ring?
3. What fruit could go outside the circle?
4. How else could you sort the fruit inside the circle?

Scholastic Data Handling   Year 1

PHOTOCOPIABLE   SCHOLASTIC
www.scholastic.co.uk

Fruit and vegetables

Lesson 5

Mathematics learning objectives
Framework:
- **U&A:** Answer a question by selecting and using suitable equipment, and sorting information, shapes or objects; display results using tables and pictures.
- **U&A:** Describe ways of solving puzzles and problems, explaining choices and decisions orally or using pictures.
- **HD:** Use diagrams to sort objects into groups according to a given criterion; suggest a different criterion for grouping the same objects.

NC: Ma2, 1a-c; Ma2, 1g; Ma2, 5a-b

PSHE learning objective (NC)
- **3a:** Understand how to make simple choices that improve their health and wellbeing.

Vocabulary
Count, sort, vote

Resources
- A range of fruit and vegetables (real or plastic models), 'Fruit' and 'Vegetable' labels, sorting rings, safety scissors and glue sticks

CD-ROM slideshow:
- Activity sheets: 'Sorting ring' (enlarged to A3), 'Fruit and vegetables' (one copy for each child and one copy enlarged to A3) and 'Sorting food' (also p15)

Introduction
Talk with the children about the importance of fruit and vegetables in a healthy diet. Ask two children to say what they eat for breakfast/lunch/dinner and to say whether they think their choices are healthy. Ask the class what choices they can make to make their diet more healthy.

Show the class the fruit and vegetables. Explain that you would like the children to help you to decide where each piece belongs. Show the enlarged copy of the activity sheet 'Sorting ring' and place the 'Fruit' label just inside the ring. Hold up, for example, an apple, and ask: *Where does this belong?* Repeat for the other fruit and vegetables until all are sorted. Now repeat this activity, removing the label and replacing it with 'Vegetables'. Ask questions such as:
- *Why does the banana fit outside the ring?*
- *Why does the carrot fit inside the ring?*
- *What is the same about all the things inside/outside the ring?*

Children's task
Provide each child with a copy of the activity sheet 'Fruit and vegetables' and ask them to colour and cut out the pictures at the bottom of the sheet. They should then sort the pictures so that all the round fruit and vegetables are inside the circle and the other fruit and vegetables are outside the circle. Ask them to discuss their sorting with a partner and discuss any differences. If time permits, ask them to draw at least one other fruit or vegetable on the inside of the circle and one outside the circle.

Differentiation
More confident: Challenge the children to think of two more kinds of fruit and two more vegetables to draw onto their diagram. Ask them to explain their choices and how they decided where to draw them.
Less confident: Ask an adult to work with a small group, using an A3 enlargement of the activity sheet 'Fruit and vegetables'. The children, with prompting from the adult, decide where each fruit and vegetable belongs.

Review
Display your A3 enlargement of the activity sheet 'Fruit and vegetables', with the pictures already cut out and placed. Ask questions such as:
- *How else could we sort these fruit and vegetables?*
- *How many are inside the ring?*
- *What is special about these picture types of fruit and vegetables?*
- *Which was the most difficult fruit or vegetable to place?*
- *Think of another way to sort these.*

Now try this...
Children can sort other foodstuffs:
- breakfast cereals (sweet/not sweet; chocolatey/no chocolate)
- nuts
- dried fruit.

CD-ROM follow-up material
Display the activity sheet 'Sorting food' on the whiteboard. Ask the children to work in groups to discuss and answer the questions.

Lesson 5

Sorting food

- Look at the sorting ring. It shows how some food has been sorted.
- Answer the questions below.

1. What can you see inside the circle?
2. What is outside the circle?
3. How do you think these foods were sorted?
4. What label could we give this sorting diagram?

Chicken and eggs

Lesson 6

Mathematics learning objectives
Framework:
- **U&A:** Answer a question by selecting and using suitable equipment, and sorting information, shapes or objects; display results using tables and pictures.
- **U&A:** Describe ways of solving puzzles and problems, explaining choices and decisions orally or using pictures.

NC: Ma2, 1a-c; Ma2, 1g; Ma2, 5a-b

Science learning objectives (NC)
- **Sc2, 1a:** Know the differences between things that are living and things that have never been alive.
- **Sc2, 1b:** Understand that animals, including humans, move, feed, grow, use their senses and reproduce.
- **Sc2, 1c:** Relate life processes to animals and plants found in the local environment.

Vocabulary
Count, greatest, least, list, pictogram

Resources
- Toy chicken, plastic eggs

CD-ROM slideshow:
- Activity sheets: 'Eggs every day', 'Our chicken and eggs' (also p17), 'Feed the ducks' and 'Our class birthdays' (enlarged to A2)
- Image: 'Hen with eggs'
- Pictogram tool
- Interactive table: 'Eggs data collection' (enlarged to A3)
- Word® file: 'Our class birthdays'

Introduction
Begin this work on a Monday. Display the image 'Hen with eggs' from the CD-ROM; ask the children if they have seen hens lay their eggs and discuss. Introduce the toy chicken. Before the children arrive each morning, decide how many eggs the chicken has 'laid', between 0 and 6. Display the chicken with that many eggs beside her. As the children come into the classroom, ask them to go to the chicken and count the eggs for that day. Once they are sitting down ask:
- How many eggs are there today?
- (From Tuesday) Is that more or fewer than yesterday?
- How many eggs do you think the chicken will lay tomorrow?

On Tuesday morning put out a different number of eggs. Use the children's counting ability to determine the range of counts of eggs across the week. Show the children the interactive table 'Eggs data collection'. Explain that they will record the number of eggs laid each day.

Children's task
Provide each child with a copy of the activity sheet 'Eggs every day'. Each morning after the children have counted the eggs they complete that day's pictogram column to show the number of eggs. Ask:
- How many eggs were there yesterday?
- Did the chicken lay more/fewer eggs today or yesterday?

Differentiation
More confident: Challenge the children to keep a running total of how many eggs the chicken has laid. Encourage them to count on from the previous day's total in order to find the running total. Provide counting materials if they struggle with the count.
Less confident: Suggest to the children that they touch, count and move each egg, coordinating the touch and saying the number name.

Review
On Friday, after the eggs are counted, complete the interactive table 'Eggs data collection' and ask each child to complete their pictogram. Now introduce the pictogram tool. With the children's help make a pictogram of the number of eggs laid each day, using the egg icon or coloured counters to represent the eggs. Ask questions such as:
- How many eggs did we count on Wednesday?
- On which day was there the greatest number of eggs? How many eggs was that?
- On which day was there the least number of eggs? How many eggs was that?
- Which day had more/less than three eggs?

Display the activity sheet 'Our chicken and eggs' and discuss the questions with the children.

Now try this...
Ask the children to count how many eggs they eat in one week. Make a class pictogram of the results.

CD-ROM follow-up material
There are further sheets on the CD-ROM for the children to use: 'Feed the ducks' and 'Our class birthdays'. Adapt your questions to suit these pictograms.

Scholastic Data Handling Year 1

Lesson 6

Our chicken and eggs
This is how many eggs our chicken laid

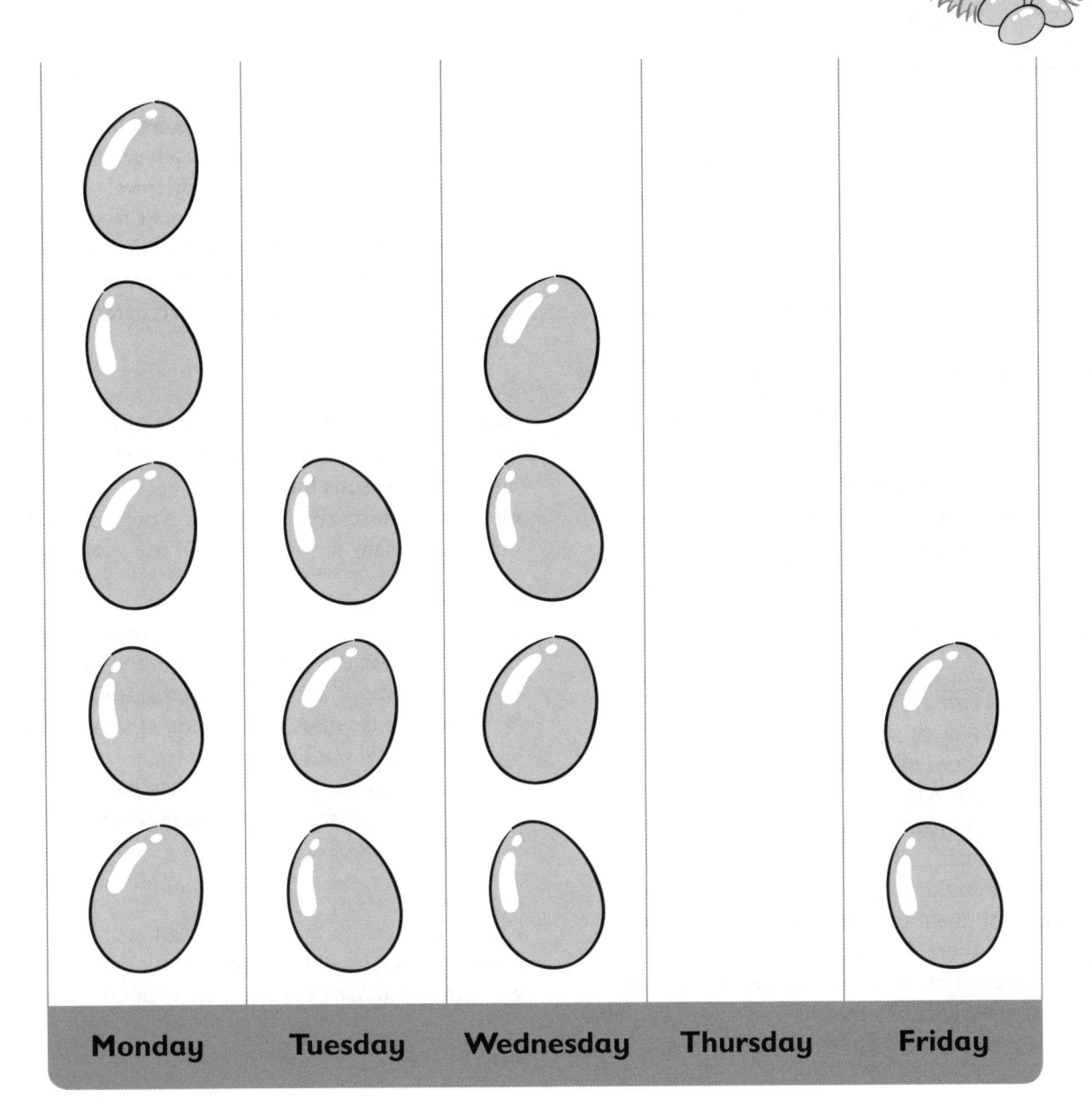

Monday	Tuesday	Wednesday	Thursday	Friday

1. Is this pictogram the same as yours?
2. Why do you think that is?
3. How many more eggs were there on Monday than on Wednesday?
4. What do you think happened to the chicken on Thursday?

Scholastic Data Handling Year 1

PHOTOCOPIABLE
SCHOLASTIC
www.scholastic.co.uk

Holiday travel

Lesson 7

Mathematics learning objectives
Framework:
- **HD:** Answer a question by recording information in lists and tables; present outcomes using practical resources, pictures, block graphs or pictograms.

NC: Ma2, 5a-b

Geography learning objectives (NC)
- **5b:** Recognise how the environment may be improved and sustained (for example, by restricting the number of cars).

Vocabulary
Count, fewer, more, table, vote

Resources
CD-ROM slideshow:
- Activity sheets: 'Our favourite transport – 1' (also p19), 'Holiday travel table' (enlarged to A3 for each group), 'Holiday travel pictogram' (enlarged to A3 for each group), and 'Our favourite transport – 2'

Introduction
Explain to the children that in this lesson they will be considering how they travel to go on holiday. Begin with a discussion about the environment; ask children what forms of transport they think help the environment, and why they think that. Display the activity sheet 'Our favourite transport – 1', ask the questions and discuss the data. Ask:
- *Which of the forms of transport is kindest to the environment? Why do you think that?*
- *Which of the forms of transport has the most impact on the environment? Why do you think that?*
- *What things can you do in your life to help the environment?*

Show the children the activity sheet 'Holiday travel table'. Read with them the different forms of holiday transport listed there. Children may want to add other ideas, such as bicycles, on a separate sheet. Now, for each type of transport, ask the children to put up their hands if they have used this to go on holiday, and write the number of children who have in the 'How many' column. Some children may have used two or more modes of transport, such as car and plane. When the table is complete, ask questions such as:
- *Which form of transport was the most popular?*
- *Which was the least popular?*
- *Which is more popular than ...?*
- *Why do you think that?*

Children's task
Divide the class into groups and provide each group with the activity sheets 'Holiday travel table' and 'Holiday travel pictogram'. Ask each group to work together to complete the 'Holiday travel table': they can add additional forms of transport to the table if required. They should then use the information from the table to create a group 'Holiday travel pictogram'. Suggest that they compare their pictograms once completed.

Differentiation
More confident: Encourage the children to include all the forms of transport that they each used and to discuss the reasons for each.
Less confident: Work with this group to help them to count how many for each form of transport.

Review
Each group's pictogram will be different. Display one or two and discuss the differences with the class. Ask the children questions about their pictogram such as:
- *Which was the most popular form of transport? Why do you think that was?*
- *Which is your favourite form of transport? Is this the same as the most popular on your pictogram? Why do you think that is?*

Now try this...
Repeat the activity, this time asking the children to give information on how they travel to visit their grandparents, go to the swimming pool or visit a famous landmark.

CD-ROM follow-up material
Display the activity sheet 'Our favourite transport – 2' from the CD-ROM. Complete the final column with the class, then discuss the differences between the two sets of data. Ask children to explain their choices, with an emphasis on environment and sustainability.

Our favourite transport – 1

■ This table shows the favourite forms of transport of the children from Mount Street Primary School.
■ Look at the table, then answer the questions.

Transport	Mount Street Primary School
car	10
walk	3
bus	4
train	5
plane	6

1. How many children like to travel by train more than walking?
2. Which is the most popular form of transport?
3. Which is the least popular form of transport?
4. How many fewer children like to go by bus than by plane?

Musical instruments

Lesson 8

Mathematics learning objectives
Framework:
- **HD:** Answer a question by recording information in lists and tables; present outcomes using practical resources, pictures, block graphs or pictograms.
- **HD:** Use diagrams to sort objects into groups according to a given criterion; suggest a different criterion for grouping the same objects.

NC: Ma2, 5a-b

Music learning objectives (NC)
- **1b:** Play tuned and untuned instruments.
- **4c:** Learn how sounds can be made in different ways (for example, vocalising, clapping, by musical instruments, in the environment, and described using given and invented signs and symbols).

Vocabulary
Count, group, list, set, sort, table

Resources
- Musical instruments such as triangles, drums, tambourines, maracas, glockenspiels, and so on

CD-ROM slideshow:
- Activity sheets: 'Musical instruments' (also p21), 'How are they played?' 1 and 2 (enlarged to A3)
- Images: 'Musical instruments' 1 and 2

Introduction
Display the image 'Musical instruments 1' from the CD-ROM. Talk about the instruments and how they are played. Show the children the activity sheet 'Musical instruments' on the whiteboard and discuss. Display the physical musical instruments. Check that the children know the name of each one. Invite a child to the front of the class to demonstrate how to make a sound with, for example, the triangle. Discuss whether this is a tap or a shake. Repeat this for another instrument. Ask:
- How does this instrument make its sound?
- Is there another way to play this instrument?

Give each child an A3 copy of 'How are they played? – 1' and display on the interactive whiteboard: explain that this is a data-collection table which lists the properties of the musical instruments. Read together 'shake' and 'tap'. Discuss where the triangle belongs on the table (tap). Invite the children to look at the instruments and decide whether there is an instrument that would fit 'shake' and where this would go on the table.

Children's task
Ask the children to work in small groups with a set of musical instruments. Explain that they should quietly try each instrument for themselves, decide how it makes its sound, then sketch it onto the activity sheet 'How are they played? – 1' in the appropriate place.

Differentiation
More confident: When the set work is finished, the children can explore other ways of making sounds with the instruments. They can make their own data-collection table in order to record their findings.

Less confident: Decide whether to ask an adult to work with this group. Ask the adult to encourage the children to explain where each instrument will fit onto their table.

Review
Hold up each instrument in turn and ask the children questions such as:
- How does this instrument make its sound?
- Where would it fit on our table?
- Is there another way to make the sound?

Use an A3 printout of 'How are they played? – 1' to quickly sketch the instrument in its place. When all the instruments have been categorised, ask questions about how the sounds are made.

Now try this...
The children could sort musical instruments by:
- shape
- whether they are warm to the touch or cold (such as metal like a triangle)
- their own suggested criteria.

CD-ROM follow-up material
Display the image 'Musical instruments 2' from the CD-ROM. Give each group a copy of the activity sheet 'How are they played? – 2' to discuss and complete. Ask the children to think of other ways the instruments could be sorted.

Lesson 8

Musical instruments

- This table shows how musical instruments are played.
- Look at the table, then answer the questions.

How it is played	Instruments
use your hand	
use a stick	
blow	

1. What other instruments could we add to this table?
2. What other instruments do we use?
3. Where would they fit on this table?
4. How many metal instruments can you think of?

Melting ice

Lesson 9

Mathematics learning objectives
Framework:
- **U&A**: Answer a question by selecting and using suitable equipment, and sorting information, shapes or objects; display results using tables and pictures.
- **U&A**: Describe ways of solving puzzles and problems, explaining choices and decisions orally or using pictures.
- **HD**: Answer a question by recording information in lists and tables; present outcomes using practical resources, pictures, block graphs or pictograms.
- **Measuring**: Use vocabulary related to time.

NC: Ma2, 1a-c; Ma2, 1g; Ma2, 5a-b; Ma3, 4a

Science learning objectives (NC)
- **Sc3, 2b**: Explore and describe the way some everyday materials (for example, water, chocolate, bread, clay) change when they are heated or cooled.

Vocabulary
Block graph, list, minute, table, time

Resources
- Ice cubes, saucers, stopwatches or clocks that read in minutes (one for each group)
- **CD-ROM slideshow:**
- Activity sheets: 'Walk around the field' (also p23) and 'Melting ice' (one copy for each group and one copy enlarged to A3)
- Image: 'Seedling growth'
- Block graph tool

Introduction
Display the block graph on the activity sheet 'Walk around the field'. Discuss the experiment these children undertook and answer the questions. Ask the children to notice how the findings from the experiment were recorded (on a block graph).

Explain that the class are going to carry out an experiment to find out how long it takes an ice cube to melt in different places around the school. Ask the children for suggestions. They may suggest leaving it on top of a radiator, outside or in the classroom. Provide each group with a stopwatch or clock and discuss how this works and what it is reading. Introduce the word 'minute'. Now display the A3 copy of the activity sheet 'Melting ice'. Discuss how they will record each of their findings.

Children's task
Place the children into small groups and provide each group with a copy of the activity sheet 'Melting ice'. Have the first group place an ice cube onto a saucer on the table and start their stopwatches. They note how long it takes to melt, stop the timer and read and record how many minutes this has taken (children may need help with this). Another group can start with an ice cube on a saucer on a radiator, and so on. If time permits each group should time each of the three experiments on the sheet. Explain that once they have completed the three suggestions they could think of other places to try and add these to the activity sheet.

Differentiation
More confident: Encourage the children to read the stopwatch for themselves.
Less confident: Decide whether to ask an adult to work with this group. They can make a group record of their work.

Review
Review the children's findings together. Make a class record of the times taken using the A3 copy of 'Melting ice', or use the tools from the CD-ROM to annotate the PDF on the whiteboard. Ask questions such as:
- *Did all the ice cubes melt in the same time on the radiator/outside…? Why?*
- *Where did the ice cubes melt fastest/slowest?*
- *Why do you think that was?*

Now display the block graph tool. Set this up with the three headings of 'Outside', 'On the table' and 'On the radiator'. Choose one group's record and enter their data. Discuss what the children see. Ask questions such as:
- *Which place has the most blocks? Why?*
- *Which blocks show the shortest time? Why?*

Now try this…
Ask the children to put an ice cube into a cold drink at home and time how long it takes to melt.

CD-ROM follow-up material
Display the image 'Seedling growth' and discuss what a seed needs to grow (water and light). Ask the children to collect data and make their own block graph for growing a seed. They can use uniform non-standard units to measure and record the growth once the seed begins to grow. Then they measure the growth each day or each week, depending on what kind of seed they have and how quickly the seedling grows.

Lesson 9

Walk around the field

- This block graph shows how long it took five children to each walk around a field.
- Look at the block graph and then answer the questions.

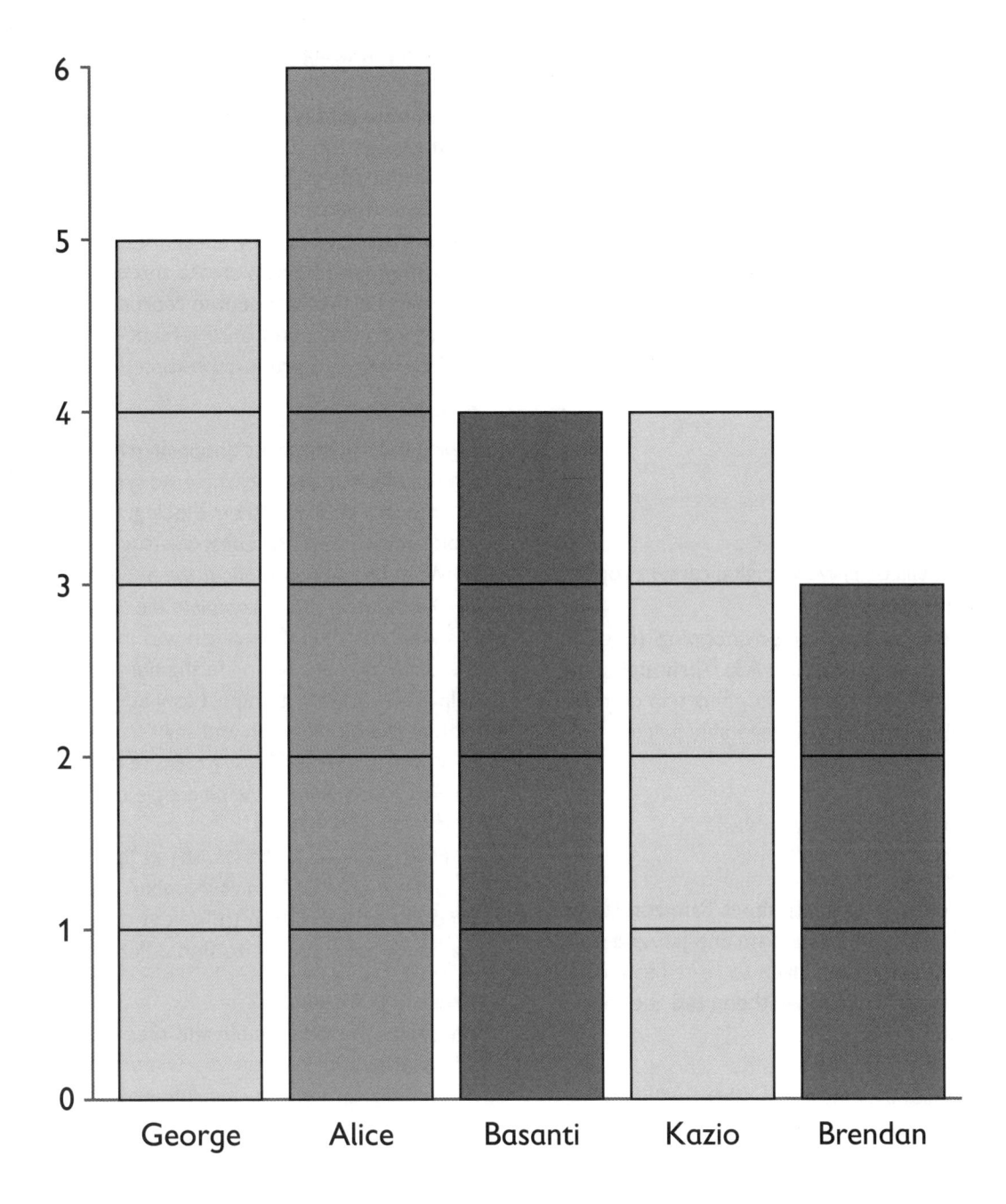

1. How long did Basanti take to walk around the field?
2. Who took the longest?
3. Who was quickest?
4. Which two children took the same time?

Shopping

Lesson 10

Mathematics learning objectives
Framework:
- **U&A**: Answer a question by selecting and using suitable equipment, and sorting information, shapes or objects; display results using tables and pictures.
- **U&A**: Describe ways of solving puzzles and problems, explaining choices and decisions orally or using pictures.
- **HD**: Answer a question by recording information in lists and tables; present outcomes using practical resources, pictures, block graphs or pictograms.

NC: Ma2, 1a-c; Ma2, 1g; Ma2, 5a-b

English learning objectives (NC)
- **En2, 2a**: Use the organisational features of non-fiction texts, including captions, illustrations, contents, index and chapters, to find information.
- **En2, 2b**: Understand that texts about the same topic may contain different information or present similar information in different ways.

Vocabulary
Block graph, list, sort

Resources
- Coloured pencils or crayons, digital camera (optional)

CD-ROM slideshow:
- Activity sheets: 'Sam and Jan go shopping' (one for each pair and one enlarged to A3), 'A shopping trip' 1 and 2 (one for each pair), 'Shopping trip completed block graph' (also p25) and 'Vegetable prices'
- Image: 'Shopping items'
- Block graph tool
- Interactive block graph: 'Vegetables'

Introduction
Display the A3 enlarged activity sheet 'Sam and Jan go shopping', read the story about Sam and Jan, and point to the pictures. Invite the children to re-tell as much of the story as they can remember, then read the story again. Ask questions such as:
- How much is the pineapple?
- Tell me the prices of some of the other fruit.

Children's task
Ask the children to work in pairs. Leave the A3 page on display and provide each pair with the activity sheets 'Sam and Jan go shopping' and 'A shopping trip' 1 and 2, and coloured pencils. Ask each pair to use the story sheet to complete the table, then use the information from the table to create a block graph.

Differentiation
More confident: Some children could create their block graph using the block graph tool in the Kids Zone on the CD-ROM: they may need help with this. If the children finish this work early, suggest that they find out what change there would be from 10p for each piece of fruit in the story. They can write this into their table.
Less confident: Discuss what the children notice about the prices as they enter these onto their table. They may need help to create the block graph. Remind the children that one square represents 1p. Decide whether to use an A3 enlargement of the block graph and to work as a group to complete this.

Review
Reveal the activity sheet 'Shopping trip completed block graph', which shows a completed graph. Ask the children to compare this with their block graph to see if they look similar. Now ask questions such as:
- What do you notice about the prices on your table?
- Did this help you to complete the block graph?

Discuss how the information was in order of price on the table. Explain that ordering numbers like this can help when making a graph. Now ask the children to look at the block graph and say:
- Which is the most/least expensive fruit?
- How much more is the pineapple than the apple? How did you work this out?
- How much less is the strawberry than the orange? How can you tell that from your graph?

Encourage the children to look at their graphs and note that they can count on to find differences.

Now try this...
Children can make a table and then block graph of prices of goods:
- in the class shop, during role play
- toys
- items on the image 'Shopping items'.

CD-ROM follow-up material
Display the activity sheet 'Vegetable prices'. Ask the children to work in pairs to answer the questions and complete a block graph using the tool in the Kids Zone. Display the interactive block graph 'Vegetables' for them to compare their graphs to.

Scholastic Data Handling Year 1

Lesson 10

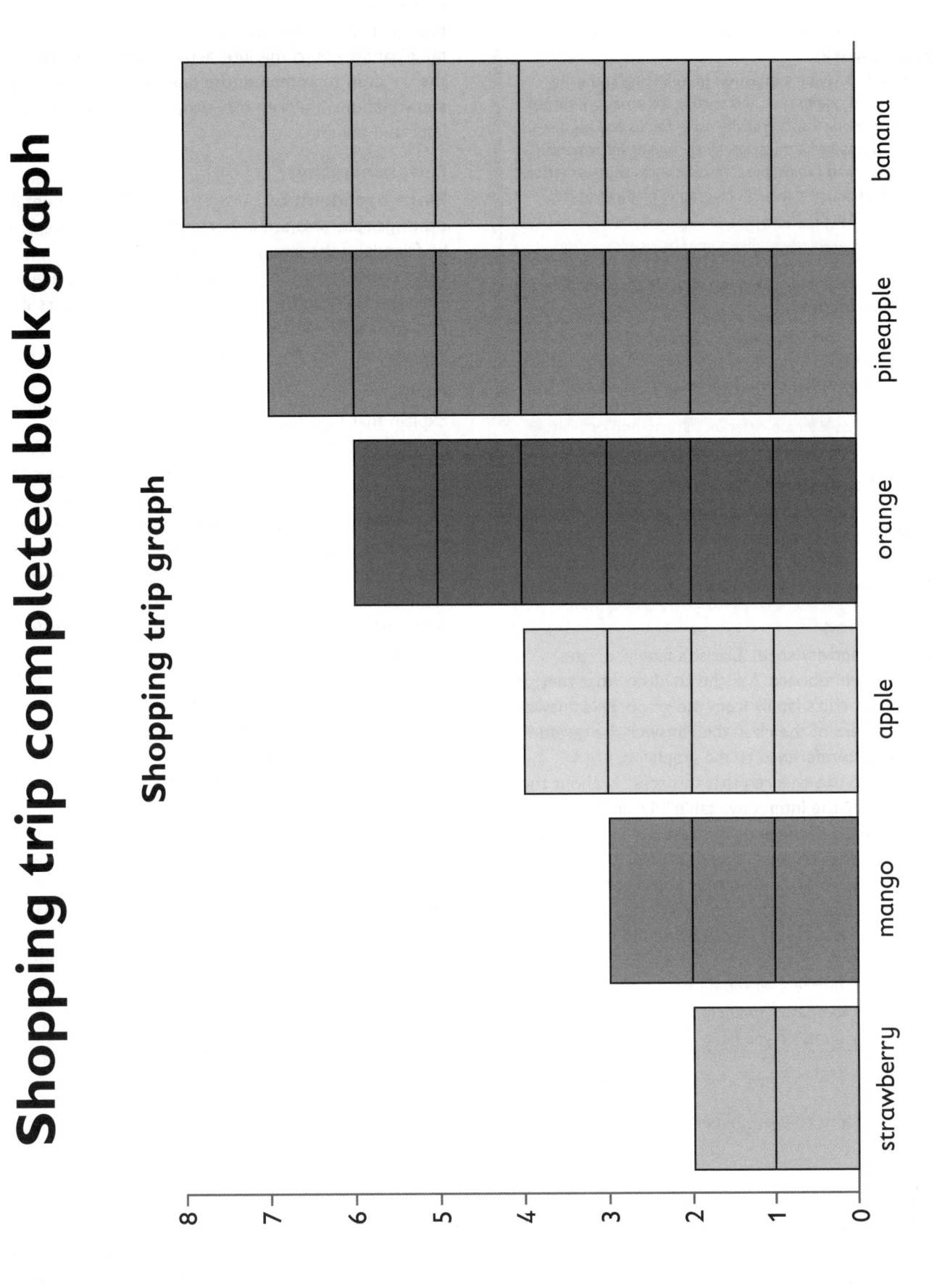

Shopping trip completed block graph

Shopping trip graph

Fruit	Count
strawberry	2
mango	3
apple	4
orange	6
pineapple	7
banana	8

Scholastic Data Handling Year 1

My family

Lesson 11

Mathematics learning objectives
Framework:
- **U&A**: Answer a question by selecting and using suitable equipment, and sorting information, shapes or objects; display results using tables and pictures.
- **HD**: Answer a question by recording information in lists and tables; present outcomes using practical resources, pictures, block graphs or pictograms.

NC: Ma2, 1g; Ma2, 5a-b

PSHE learning objective (NC)
- **4d**: Understand that family and friends should care for each other.

Vocabulary
- Block graph, count, list, set, sort, table, vote

Resources
CD-ROM slideshow:
- Activity sheets: 'Darish's family' (also p27), 'My family – table', and 'The Jones family'
- Block graph tool
- Interactive table: 'My family'

Introduction
Display the activity sheet 'Darish's family' on the interactive whiteboard. Ask the children what they can tell about Darish's family from the graph. Take answers from members of the class, then answer the questions together with reference to the graph.

Explain to the children that this topic is about their family. Display the interactive table 'My family' or give children copies of the activity sheet 'My family – table'. Ask the children to think about relatives that they have. Point out on the table where each of these could go. Children may suggest other relatives, such as step-brothers and sisters, which can be added to the chart if appropriate. Ask questions from page 27, and:
- How many brothers do you have?
- Who has more/fewer brothers than Peter?
- How many aunts do you have?

Children's task
Provide each child with the activity sheet 'My family – table' or access to the interactive table 'My family'. Ask the children to complete the table. Where there are step-relations, children may want to add these to the left-hand column.

Differentiation
More confident: Encourage the children to identify other people who are important to them. These could be friends of the family for example.

Less confident: Decide whether to work as a group. Help the children to read the words on the chart. If they find writing down the names of their relatives difficult, suggest that they put a tick for each person they think of.

Review
Explain that you would like to build a class block graph about brothers and sisters. Ask the children to calculate the total number of brothers and sisters they each have. Use the block graph tool in the slideshow on the interactive whiteboard to create a block graph. The x-axis should show the numbers 1 to 5 and 'more than 5', and the y-axis should go from 0 to 10. Ask the children to put up their hands when you say a number which will be the total of their brothers and sisters. Put these results into the table. Ask:
- Who has no brothers or sisters?
- Who has one/two/three brothers and sisters?

When the table is complete ask questions such as:
- What shall we call this table? What is it about?
- What is the largest number of brothers and sisters together?
- How many of you have this number of brothers and sisters? How can we read that from the table?
- What is the least number? How can we tell this? How many of you have this number?

Invite the more confident learners to suggest other people that could be added to their chart, and discuss the relationship.

Now try this...
In groups, research family information as part of a history or geography unit.

CD-ROM follow-up material
Display the activity sheet 'The Jones family'. Ask the children to discuss the questions in a small group. Ask each group to think of at least one additional question and discuss these together.

Lesson 11

Darish's family

■ Look at the block graph below. It shows how many family members Darish has.

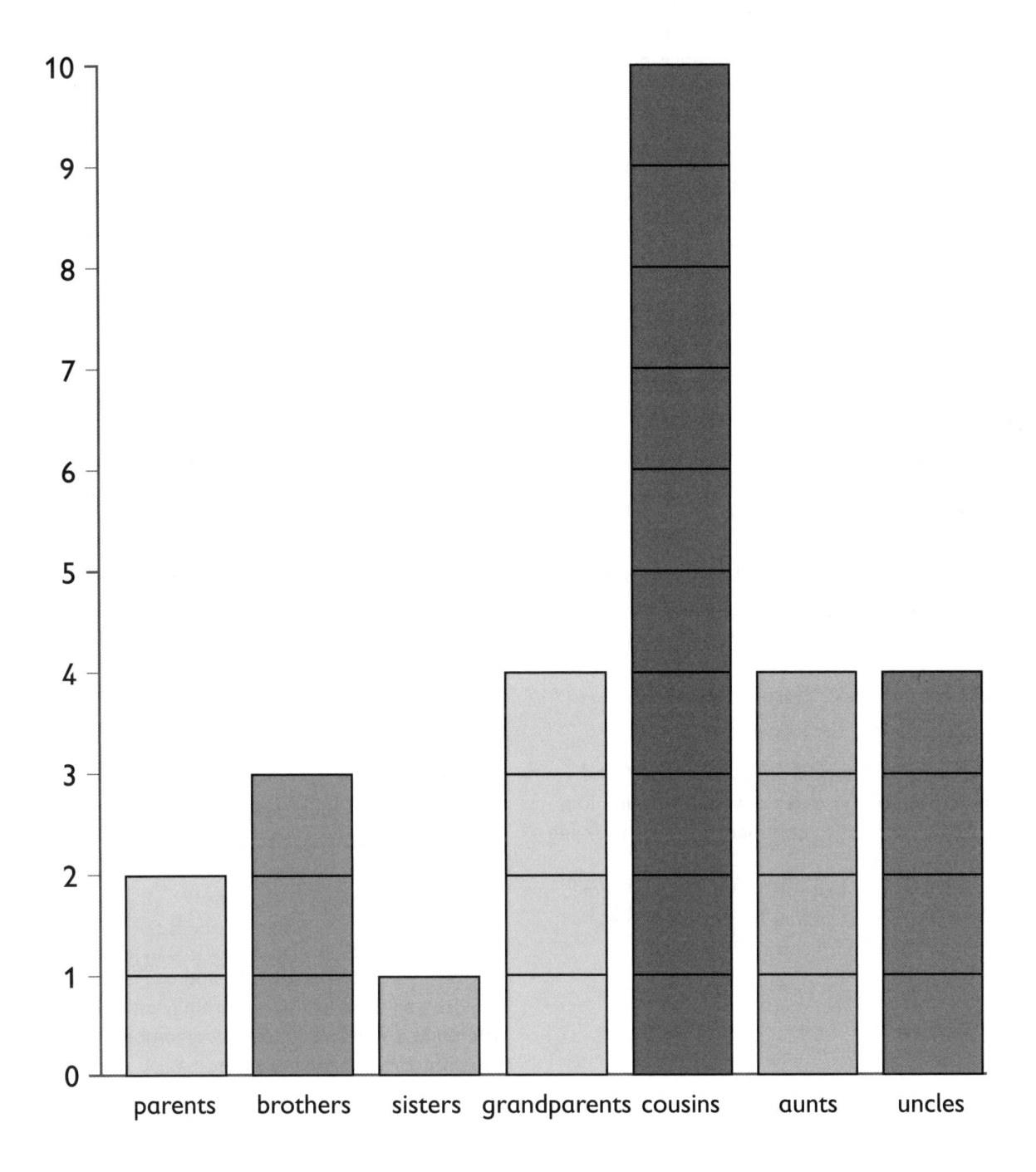

	parents	brothers	sisters	grandparents	cousins	aunts	uncles
count	2	3	1	4	10	4	4

1. How many brothers and sisters are there altogether?
2. How did you work that out?
3. How many more cousins are there than brothers and sisters?
4. Are there more aunts than uncles?

Inside my home

Lesson 12

Mathematics learning objectives
Framework:
- **U&A**: Answer a question by selecting and using suitable equipment, and sorting information, shapes or objects; display results using tables and pictures.
- **U&A**: Describe ways of solving puzzles and problems, explaining choices and decisions orally or using pictures.
- **HD**: Answer a question by recording information in lists and tables; present outcomes using practical resources, pictures, block graphs or pictograms.
- **HD**: Use diagrams to sort objects into groups according to a given criterion; suggest a different criterion for grouping the same objects.

NC: Ma2, 1a-c; Ma2, 1g; Ma2, 5a-b

PSHE learning objective (NC)
- **3a**: Learn how to make simple choices that improve their health and wellbeing.

Vocabulary
Group, set, sort

Resources
- Safety scissors, glue sticks and A3 sheets of paper

CD-ROM slideshow:
- Activity sheets: 'Inside my home' and 'Inside Jon's home' (also p29)
- Images: 'Furniture' and 'Playground items'

Introduction
Display the image 'Furniture' from the CD-ROM and discuss where each of these items would be found in a house. Invite the children to comment on what they see. Ask questions such as:
- *Name something here that you have inside your home.*
- *Is there anything on this picture that you would not expect to find inside your home? Why is that?*

Pointing to a picture:
- *Where does this go in your home?*
- *What is it used for?*

Children's task
Give each child a copy of the activity sheet 'Inside my home' and a sheet of A3 paper. Explain that you would like them to sort the pictures. Ask them to cut out the pictures, then decide which belong inside their home and where inside it. Say that everyone's sorting is likely to be different. Ask them to make their own sorting diagram on the A3 sheet of paper, then to glue the pictures onto their diagram. They should write a label for their diagram.

Differentiation
More confident: When the children have finished, suggest that they cut out another set of pictures and make a different way of recording. Suggest that all of the pictures should be on their diagram this time.

Less confident: Discuss with the children which things they have at home and where these things belong inside their home. If necessary draw a sorting ring onto the A3 sheet of paper for them.

Review
Ask the children to compare their diagrams with a partner. Encourage them to discuss how they have sorted, what decisions they made, and whether their type of sorting diagram works well. Invite a child to show their sorting diagram to the class. Ask:
- *How is it the same/different?*
- *Where did Sally put the elephant?*
- *Why do you think she did that?*

Repeat this with another child's diagram. Choose one that is more complicated, showing the items separated by the room that they belong in. Ask:
- *Why are these things together?*
- *Which room is this?*
- *Is this diagram the same or different from yours?*
- *Which do you prefer? Why is that?*

Display the activity sheet 'Inside Jon's home' and discuss how this sorting differed from their own. Answer the questions together.

Now try this...
Provide some old catalogues and magazines. Ask the children to choose a page, carefully cut out the pictures, then find a way to sort them, remembering to write a label for their sorting diagram.

CD-ROM follow-up material
Display the image 'Playground items' from the CD-ROM. Ask the children in their groups to make a list of the different ways these items could be sorted.

Lesson 12

Inside Jon's home

- Jon sorted the pictures from 'Inside my home' like this.
- Look at the diagram, then read the questions below.

1. What label would you give this diagram?
2. Where does Jon keep his laptop? Do you think that is a good idea? Why do you think that?
3. Where do you think Jon and his family watch television? What tells you this?
4. Where do you think Jon and his family eat their meals? Why do you think that?
5. Why do you think the toilet is in a box on its own? Where is yours at home?
6. Where do you think the dog lives?

Scholastic Data Handling Year 1

29

PHOTOCOPIABLE SCHOLASTIC
www.scholastic.co.uk

Lesson 13

The weather

Mathematics learning objectives
Framework:
- **U&A**: Answer a question by selecting and using suitable equipment, and sorting information, shapes or objects; display results using tables and pictures.
- **HD**: Answer a question by recording information in lists and tables; present outcomes using practical resources, pictures, block graphs or pictograms.

NC: Ma2, 1g; Ma2, 5a-b

Science learning objectives (NC)
- **Sc2, 3a**: Recognise that plants need light and water to grow.
- **Sc2, 2b**: Understand that humans and other animals need food and water to stay alive.

Vocabulary
Chart, list, table

Resources
CD-ROM slideshow:
- Activity sheets: 'Weather symbols', 'The weather this week' (also p31), 'Our weather chart' (one copy for each child and one A3 copy)
- Word® file: 'Weather for the month'

Introduction
This activity works best if begun on Monday. Discuss the weather with the children, asking questions such as:
- *What is the weather like today?*
- *What was it like yesterday?*
- *What do you think it will be like tomorrow? Why?*

Point to each of the symbols on the activity sheet 'Weather symbols' and ask:
- *What sort of weather does this show?*
- *How do you know?*

Show the children the activity sheet 'The weather this week'. Point to Monday and ask the children to read the label, then Tuesday, and so on. Look at the symbols for each day and answer the questions. Ask:
- *How hot do you think it is? Why do you think that?*
- *Is this the same one as our week? How do you know?*

Children's task
Provide each child with a copy of the activity sheet 'Our weather chart'. Explain that each day of the week they will choose a weather symbol for that day and draw it on their chart. 'Weather symbols' can be displayed while they are doing this task, to help with ideas. Each morning the children draw in a symbol to show the weather for that day. They can colour their symbol but should not take long – about five minutes in total. Keep a class chart on display. The children repeat the activity every day for a week, taking their chart home on Friday to record the weekend weather.

Differentiation
More confident: Discuss how sometimes two symbols are needed to show the weather for the day. Children can design their symbols to show a combination of weather if appropriate.

Less confident: Work together to name the days of the week, and check that the children understand where their symbol should go. Check that they understand what each symbol stands for, and that they draw theirs quickly and with reasonable accuracy.

Review
On the following Monday ask the children to compare their charts with the class one. Ask:
- *What is missing from the class chart? (Saturday's and Sunday's weather symbols.)*
- *Look at your chart. What was the weather like on Saturday? And on Sunday?*

Complete the class chart for the week. Ask, for example:
- *On how many days was the weather sunny/snowy/raining?*
- *Did we have more sunny days than …?*
- *How do you know that?*
- *What do you think the weather will be like this week?*

Ask some of the more confident learners who have drawn combined symbols for their chart to explain what they have done and why.

Now try this...
Make a weather line for the month. Use the symbols from 'Weather symbols', the day and date. The chart can be a long thin one to go across the top of the whiteboard.

CD-ROM follow-up material
Use the Word® file 'Weather for the month' from the CD-ROM for children to track the weather over a longer period.

Lesson 13

The weather this week

- This chart shows what the weather was like every day for a week.
- Look at the chart, then answer the questions.

The weather this week

Day	Weather
Monday	❄️
Tuesday	🌧️❄️
Wednesday	⛅
Thursday	🌧️
Friday	☁️

1. What time of year do you think this is?
2. What happened on Monday?
3. What happened on Tuesday?
4. What do you think happened to the snow?

Scholastic Data Handling Year 1

Lesson 14

Children's toys

Mathematics learning objectives
Framework:
- **U&A**: Answer a question by selecting and using suitable equipment, and sorting information, shapes or objects; display results using tables and pictures.
- **U&A**: Describe ways of solving puzzles and problems, explaining choices and decisions orally or using pictures.
- **HD**: Answer a question by recording information in lists and tables; present outcomes using practical resources, pictures, block graphs or pictograms.

NC: Ma2, 1a-c; Ma2, 1g; Ma2, 5a-b

History learning objective (NC)
- **1a**: Place events and objects in chronological order.

Vocabulary
Group, pictogram, set, sort

Resources
- Examples of Victorian toys, such as hoop and stick, pick-up sticks, jacks or a spinning top; examples of modern toys, particularly plastic ones; safety scissors, glue sticks and A3 sheets of paper

CD-ROM slideshow:
- Activity sheets: 'Children's toys' and 'Today's toys' (also p33)
- Image: 'At the beach'
- Venn diagram tool

Introduction
Show the children some of the Victorian toys. Discuss whether these are still used today, asking questions such as:
- Which of these toys do we still use today?
- What are these toys made from?
- Do you know how to play with them?

Explore together how the toys work. Now show the modern toys. Ask:
- What are these toys made from?
- Is that the same material as the Victorian toys?
- What is different about these toys?

Discuss how children in Victorian times did not have toys made from plastic, nor did they have toys that require batteries to make them work.

Children's task
Ask the children to cut out the pictures of Victorian toys on the activity sheet 'Children's toys'. Explain that some of these toys are still used today, but they may not look quite the same. Ask the children to find ways of sorting the toys. They should draw their own sorting diagram on an A3 sheet of paper, or use the Venn diagram tool in the Kids Zone on the CD-ROM to sort the toys. Remind them to write labels to explain the sorting.

Differentiation
More confident: Challenge the children to think of three different ways of sorting the toys. They choose one of their sorting methods, then complete the task as above.
Less confident: These children may need some help with the activity. Discuss with them how each of the Victorian toys work. If necessary, work as a group to complete the task.

Review
Begin by looking at the pictogram on the activity sheet 'Today's toys' and ask for suggestions from the children about how the toys were sorted. Answer the questions together. Next ask the children to work in pairs, then in fours, to compare their own sorting diagrams. Encourage them to ask each other questions such as:
- How did you sort these?
- What other ways did you think of?

Now invite several children, with different sorting methods and different diagrams from each other, to come out to the front. Choose confident children who will accept constructive comments. Ask questions such as:
- How do you think Jack sorted these toys?
- Is this the same way that Mia sorted her toys?
- What is different?
- What sort of diagrams have been chosen?
- Which sorting diagram do you think works best?
- Why do you think that?

Now try this...
Children collect pictures of modern toys from magazines and catalogues. They cut out the pictures and sort by different criteria, then choose their favourite sorting method and record this, drawing their own diagram. Make a list of the possible criteria.

CD-ROM follow-up material
Display the image 'At the beach' from the CD-ROM on the whiteboard. Ask the children to make a list, in groups, of the different ways the items could be sorted.

Lesson 14

Today's toys

- This pictogram shows how some toys have been sorted.
- Look at the pictogram, then answer the questions below.

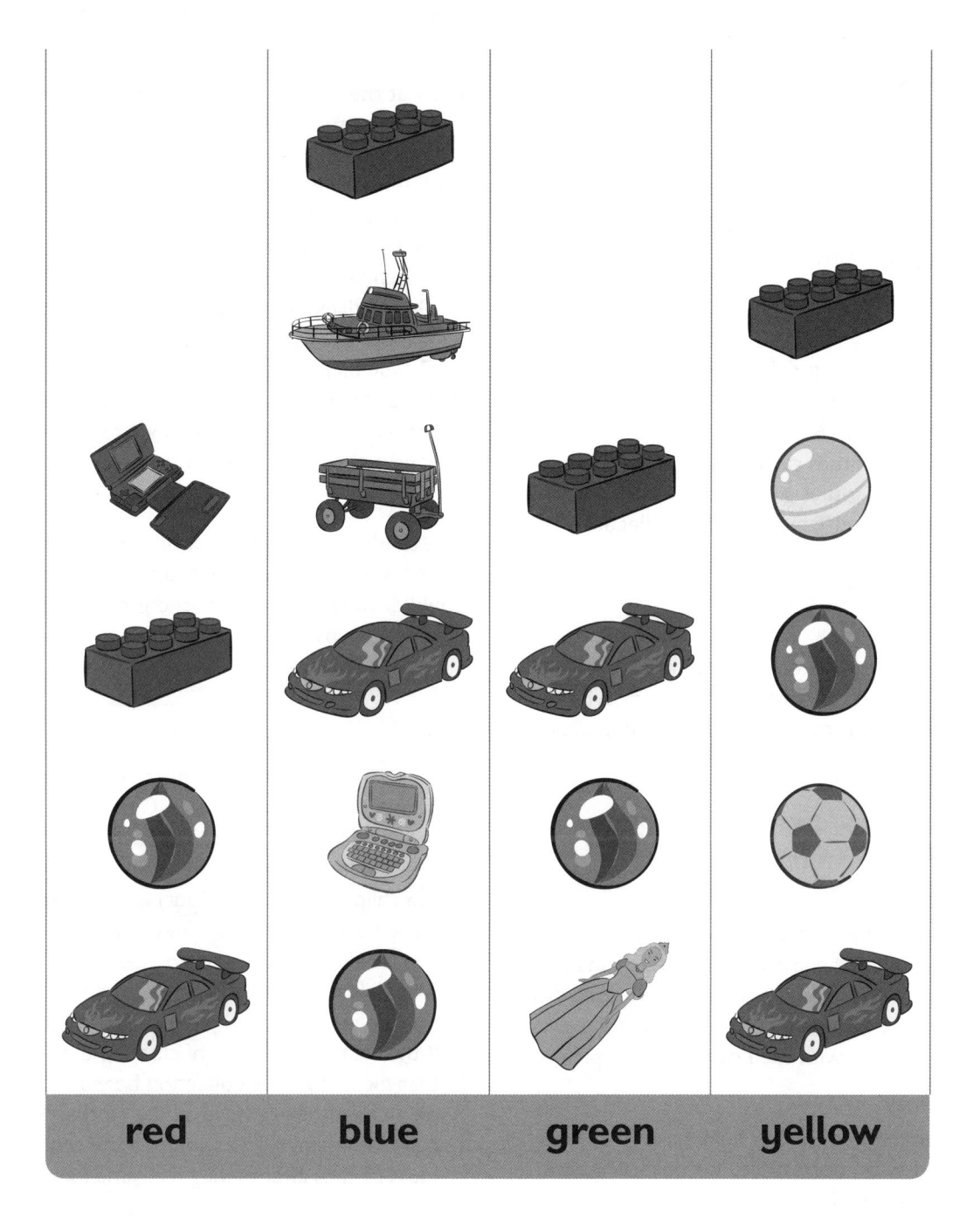

| red | blue | green | yellow |

1. How have these toys been sorted?
2. Write down one other way these toys could be sorted.
3. What other toys could be added to this pictogram?

Lesson 15

Clothes game

Mathematics learning objective
Framework:
- **HD**: Use diagrams to sort objects into groups according to a given criterion; suggest a different criterion for grouping the same objects.

NC: Ma2, 5a-b

PSHE learning objectives
- **3a**: Learn how to make simple choices that improve their health and wellbeing.
- **4b**: Listen to other people, and play and work co-operatively.

Vocabulary
Group, pictogram, sort

Resources
- 1–6 dice for each group, different coloured counter for each child and safety scissors

CD-ROM slideshow:
- Activity sheets: 'Clothes gameboard' (one A3 copy for each group), 'Clothes game tiles', 'Clothes game collection board' and 'Jamie's clothes collection' (also p35)
- Image: 'Fun activities'

Introduction
Provide each pair, or group of four, with a 'Clothes gameboard' and each child with their other activity sheets. Ask them to cut out their 'Clothes game tiles' and place them in piles in front of them. Ask questions such as:
- *Who do you think would wear these clothes?*
- *When would you wear these clothes?*

Children's task
Explain how the clothes game is to be played and check everyone understands the instructions (see opposite). Explain that they must build the tiles on their collection board as they move around the game. Remind the children to co-operate with each other as they play.

Differentiation
More confident: The children could make their own collection board, with more spaces for collecting tiles. In this case, provide additional copies of 'Clothes game tiles' for the group.

Less confident: Decide whether to ask an adult to work with this group. Children may find the idea of returning their tiles because they have landed on a cross difficult, so this should be talked through with them before the game. Alternatively, decide that if a child lands on a cross they collect no tiles for that turn.

Review
Look at the activity sheet 'Jamie's clothes collection' and discuss the questions. Ask more confident learners: *How many clothes tiles did Jamie collect altogether?* (26). Invite the children to look at their own 'Clothes game collection board.' Ask:
- *What is the largest number of one tile that you collected? Which tile was that?*
- *Do you think that everyone would collect the same number of each tile, if we carried on with the game?*
- *Do you think the game was fair?*

Ask the children to compare their collection board with a partner's. They find how many more/fewer trousers they have than their partner, and come to an agreement.

Now try this...
The children can make up a similar game with a different theme, such as favourite ice creams, fruit or toys. They could draw their own tiles and gameboard, then play it in small groups.

Game instructions
This game can be played in pairs or groups of four. Each group needs a 'Clothes gameboard', enlarged to A3. Each child needs the activity sheets 'Clothes game tiles' (which the children should cut out) and 'Clothes game collection board'. They need one dice and a different coloured counter each.
The children take turns to roll the dice and move on that number of steps from the Start position. If they land on an item of clothing they can put that tile onto their collection board. If they land on a cross they remove all the clothes from their collection board. The winner is the child with the most clothes after playing the game for ten minutes.

CD-ROM follow-up material
Display the image 'Fun activities' from the CD-ROM. Ask pairs to choose a sport or activity, from the images, and to make a list of the specific clothes they would need.

Scholastic Data Handling Year 1

Jamie's clothes collection

- This is the collection board Jamie created when he played the clothes game.
- Look at the pictogram, then answer the questions.

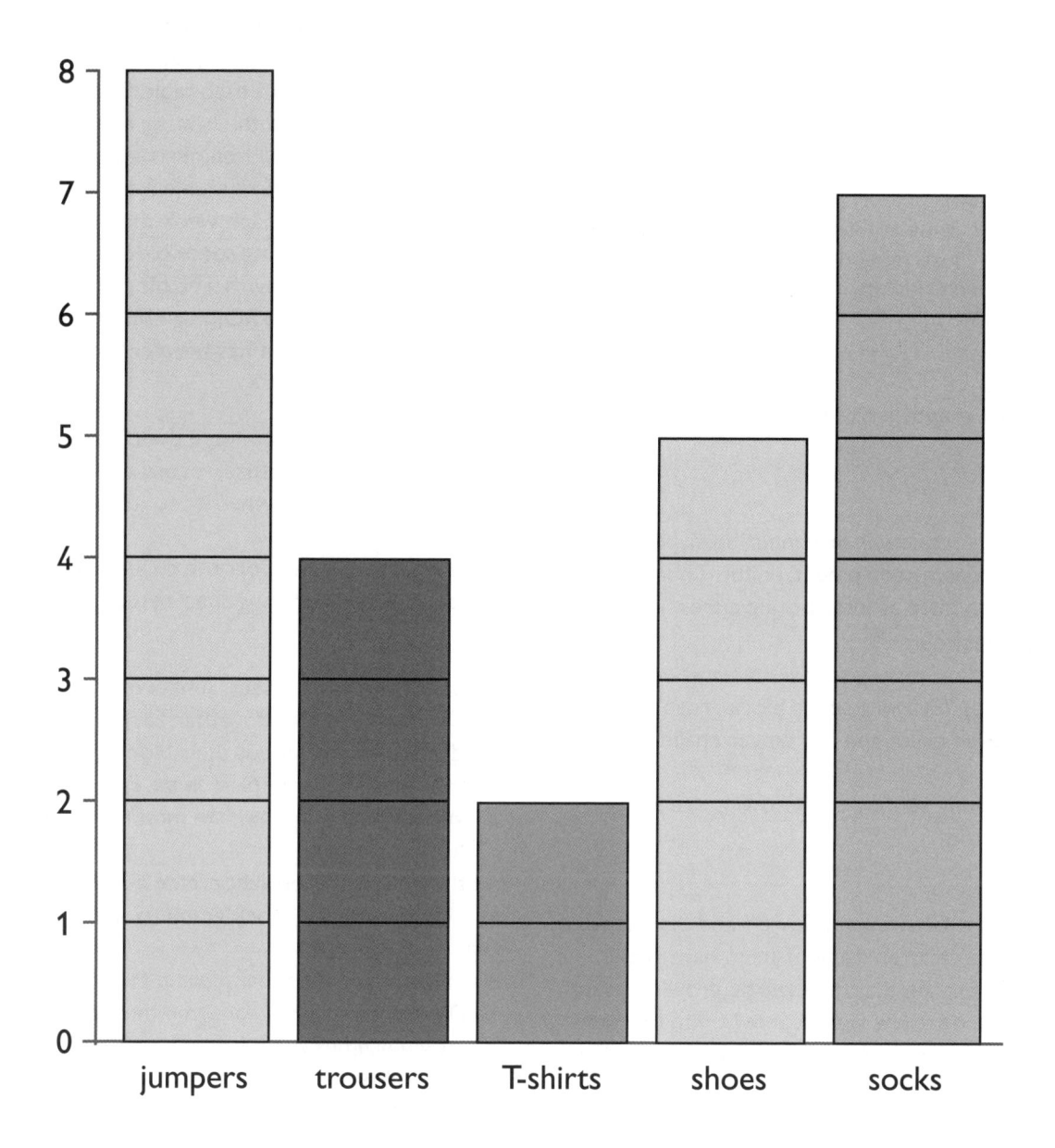

1. Are there more T-shirts than shoes?
2. Which type of clothes did Jamie collect most of?
3. What is the difference between the number of trousers and the number of socks that Jamie collected?
4. How many shoes and T-shirts did Jamie collect in total?
5. How many more socks than shoes did Jamie collect?

Lesson 16

Growing seeds

Mathematics learning objectives
Framework:
- **U&A:** Answer a question by selecting and using suitable equipment, and sorting information, shapes or objects; display results using tables and pictures.
- **HD:** Answer a question by recording information in lists and tables; present outcomes using practical resources, pictures, block graphs or pictograms.

NC: Ma2, 1g; Ma2, 5a-b

Science learning objectives (NC)
- **Sc2, 3a:** Recognise that plants need light and water to grow.
- **Sc2, 3b:** Recognise and name the leaf, flower, stem and root of flowering plants.
- **Sc2, 3c:** Understand that seeds grow into flowering plants.

Vocabulary
Count, block graph, list, table

Resources
- Seeds, such as sunflower or runner bean; pots, compost, gardening equipment; uniform non-standard units of length, such as interlocking cubes

CD-ROM slideshow:
- Activity sheets: 'Growing seeds – table' (two copies for each child), 'Growing seeds block graph' (two copies for each child) and 'Sunflower challenge' (also p37)
- Images: 'Growing sunflower'; 'Growing seeds'
- Block graph tool

Introduction
Display the image 'Growing sunflower' and discuss what it shows. Ask the children if any of them have grown plants at home. Explain that they will be growing some seeds during the next few weeks. Show them the seeds and explain which plant they should grow. Explain that each group will grow seeds outside, with plenty of light, and also some seeds in the dark. They will check each week to find out how much their seeds have grown. They will also need to water them regularly, under supervision, so that the seeds are not overwatered. Plant the seeds as a group task with adult support. Each pot should be labelled with the names of the children.

Place one pot in a dark place, such as a cupboard, and the other one in the light. Once the plants are sturdy, decide whether to plant the ones in the light outside.

Children's task
Each week the children measure their plants. They keep separate records for the seeds in the light from those in the dark, using two copies of the activity sheet 'Growing seeds – table'. They should complete the sentences at the top of each table first, to say whether the plant is growing in the light or the dark, and how it was measured. The children measure the plant grown in the light and complete the table for this, then measure the plant in the dark. Each week they add a column of blocks to their 'Growing seeds block graph' activity sheet to show the growth. The block graph tool in the Kids Zone on the CD-ROM can be used to build a graph once all the data has been collected.

Differentiation
More confident: Encourage the children to work independently to measure, record and make their block graphs. Decide whether to introduce measuring in centimetres.

Less confident: Support the children in both measuring and recording their results.

Review
Look at the activity sheet 'Sunflower challenge' and answer the questions together. Each week ask the children questions about their block graphs such as:
- *How much has your plant in the light/dark grown?*
- *Whose plant has grown the most/least? Why do you think that was?*

At the end of this project create a graph of the results as a class, using the block graph tool in the slideshow. Ask:
- *In which week did your plant in the light grow the most?*
- *Did your plant in the dark grow the most in this week too?*
- *How much has your plant in the light grown altogether?*
- *How tall is the tallest plant?*
- *Why do you think the plants in the dark did not grow well?*
- *What do plants need in order to grow tall and strong?*

Now try this...
Measure and record the children's heights at half-termly intervals.

CD-ROM follow-up material
View the image 'Growing seeds' and ask the children to take turns to describe to a partner what is happening.

Scholastic Data Handling Year 1

Sunflower challenge

- Look at this block graph. It shows the height of some sunflowers.
- Answer the questions below.

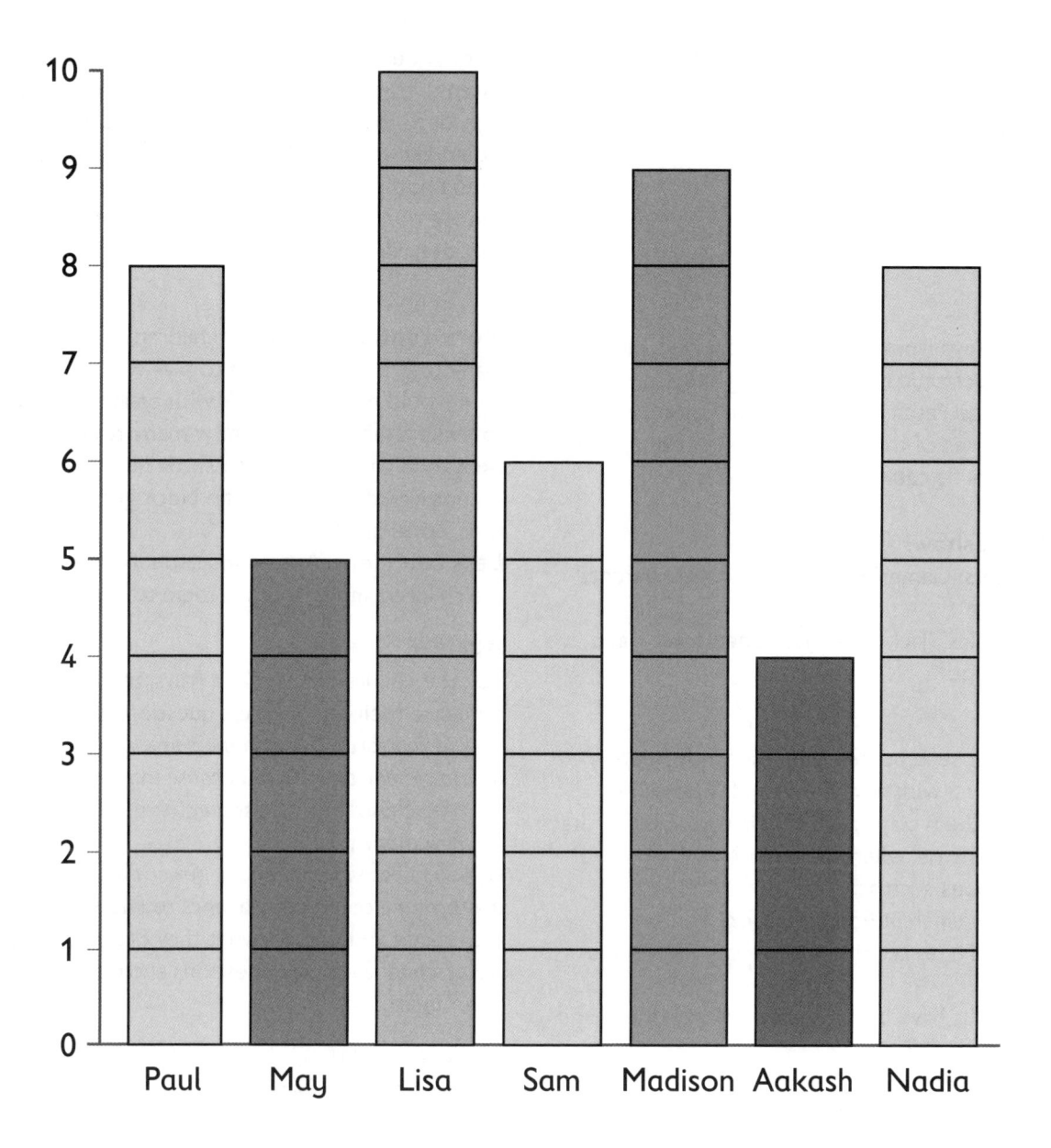

1. Who won the challenge?
2. Who came next?
3. Which two children had sunflowers that were the same height?
4. Whose sunflower was shortest?
5. How much taller was Lisa's sunflower than May's?
6. How much shorter was Aakash's sunflower than Nadia's?

Our parents' toys

Lesson 17

Mathematics learning objective
Framework:
- **HD:** Answer a question by recording information in lists and tables; present outcomes using practical resources, pictures, block graphs or pictograms.

NC: Ma2, 5a-b

History learning objective (NC)
- **1b:** Use common words and phrases relating to the passing of time (for example: before, after, a long time ago, past).

Vocabulary
Block graph, count, group, list, sort, vote

Resources
- Selection of toys from parents (for example, model cars, early electronic toys such as BigTrak, Care Bears, Cabbage Patch Kids®, My Little Pony, Glo Worm); pictures of toys used by parents from printed or online catalogues; safety scissors, glue sticks

CD-ROM slideshow:
- Activity sheets: 'Games' (also p39) and 'Our parents' toys that I like'
- Images: 'Marbles', 'Jacks', 'Old fashioned toys' 1 and 2
- Block graph tool

Introduction
Before beginning, send home a request for any toys that parents played with as children and, if possible, photographs of them playing with their toys. Display the toys and demonstrate, where possible, how they were used. Ask questions such as:
- *How are these different from your toys?*
- *Would you like a toy like this to play with? Why do you think that?*

If any photographs have been provided display these and ask questions such as:
- *Do you play like this today?*
- *Why do you think that is?*
- *Can you think of any other toys that your parents might have played with?*

Label the toys that the children have brought in with their names and what it is. Show the images of the toys from the CD-ROM. Ask which of these the children play with today.

Children's task
Display the activity sheet 'Games'. Ask the children if they know the games, and if they have played them. Answer the questions together.

Provide each child with the activity sheet 'Our parents' toys that I like'. Ask the children to draw the toys onto the sheet, sorting these into toys that they would like to play with, inside the circle, and toys they would not like to play with, outside the circle. Then they choose their favourite and write a sentence to explain why they like this toy.

Differentiation
More confident: Ask the children to count how many toys they would like to play with, and how many they would not. They work with others in their group to make a table to show how many toys each of them likes, then another table to show how many they each do not like; they can use the block graph tool in the Kids Zone on the CD-ROM.

Less confident: Ask an adult to talk about the toys with the children and encourage them to explain their choices.

Review
Ask the children to work in pairs, then in fours, to compare their sorting. Ask questions such as:
- *Did you sort the toys in the same way as your partner?*
- *How many toys did you choose that were the same?*
- *Who chose the greatest number of toys to play with? How many was that?*
- *Who chose more than … /fewer than … to play with?*

Invite more confident learners to show the tables that they made and explain what they did. Encourage the other children to ask questions such as: *Who liked more/fewer than…?*

Now try this...
Children can try sorting:
- toys from catalogues (in the same way)
- outdoor toys, into those they have tried and those they have not tried (pictures can be found in early learning catalogues).

CD-ROM follow-up material
Ask the children to agree on five games then find out how many of their classmates like to play each one. Using the block graph tool in the slideshow, make a graph of the their results.

Lesson 17

Games

- This block graph shows which games some children like playing.
- Look at the graph, then answer the questions.

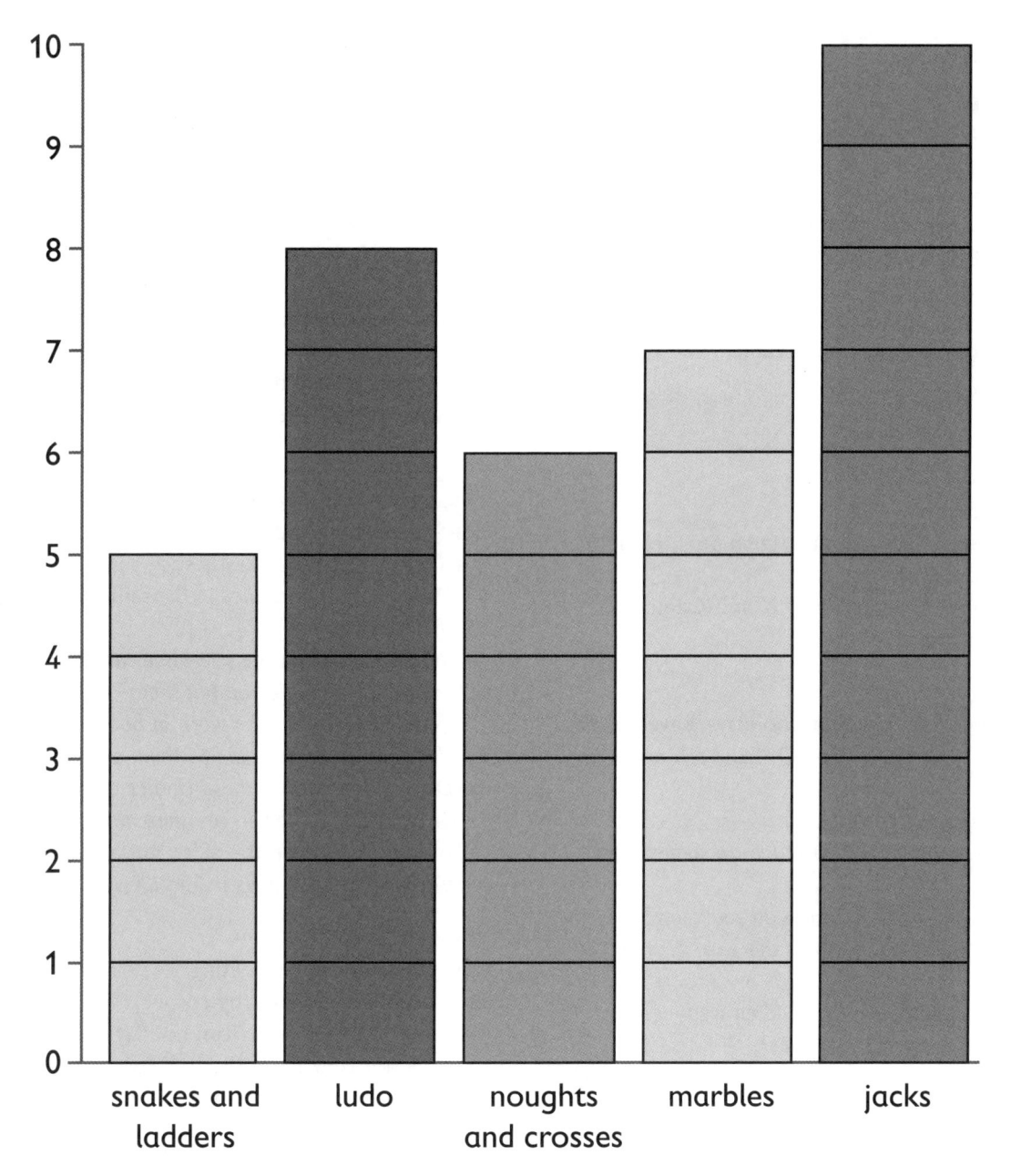

1. Which game is the most popular?
2. How many more children liked *marbles* than *snakes and ladders*?
3. How many fewer children liked *noughts and crosses* than *jacks*?
4. How many more liked *ludo* than *snakes and ladders*?
5. Which is your favourite of these games?

Holidays

Lesson 18

Mathematics learning objectives
Framework:
- **U&A**: Answer a question by selecting and using suitable equipment, and sorting information, shapes or objects; display results using tables and pictures.
- **HD**: Use diagrams to sort objects into groups according to a given criterion; suggest a different criterion for grouping the same objects.

NC: Ma2, 1g; Ma2, 5a-b

Geography learning objectives (NC)
- **3a**: Identify and describe what places are like (for example, in terms of landscape, jobs, weather).
- **3d**: Recognise how places compare with other places (for example, compare the local area with places elsewhere in the United Kingdom).

Vocabulary
Block graph, group, set, sort, table

Resources
- Safety scissors and glue sticks

CD-ROM slideshow:
- Activity sheets: 'Our holidays' (also p41), 'Holiday clothes' and 'Holiday sorting'
- Images: 'Skiing', 'Walking', 'Beach' and 'Camping'
- Block graph tool

Introduction
Explain that this lesson is about holidays. Reveal each of the four images from the CD-ROM and ask questions such as:
- *What do you see in the picture?*
- *Where do you think it is? Do you know somewhere like this?*
- *What would you do there? How do you know?*
- *What time of year do you think this was? Why do you think that?*
- *What sort of clothes are the children wearing?*
- *What is special about the clothes?*
- *Would they wear these clothes in the winter/summer? Why/why not?*

Display the activity sheet 'Our holidays'; review the information and discuss and answer the questions.

Children's task
Provide each child with a copy of the activity sheets 'Holiday clothes' and 'Holiday sorting'. Read together the labels for the two columns: 'Summer holiday' and 'Winter holiday'. Ask them to cut out the picture tiles quickly and neatly and to sort them into the table. If there is time, the children can draw more clothes to go into each column. Invite them to discuss their decisions with a partner.

Differentiation
More confident: Challenge the children to add two columns to the 'Holiday sorting' table (they may need to use an extra page), so that each column corresponds with one of the four images from the CD-ROM. They can sort the clothes from the 'Holiday clothes' page, and any other clothes they can think of, into the four columns.

Less confident: Encourage the children to sort the clothes before they begin to stick them into the sorting table. Ask them to explain their sorting.

Review
Display the completed sorting tables of a couple of children and ask the class to compare this with their own sorting. Ask questions such as:
- *Did you sort the clothes in the same way as this?*
- *What is different?*
- *Why do you think the sunglasses are in the winter column? Where did you put them?* (Elicit the fact that sunglasses can be worn at both locations.)
- *What other clothes did you think of?*
- *Do you think any of these clothes could be worn on both holidays? Why do you think that?* (Some children may comment on the skirt, but a skirt could be worn in the evenings inside a hotel in the winter.)

Now try this...
The children can try sorting:
- pictures of clothes (by colour)
- pictures of resorts, from holiday brochures (by how hot they think the holidays will be, or by whether the holidays are at the beach or inland).

CD-ROM follow-up material
Find out where the children went for their holiday. Use the block graph tool in the slideshow to create a graph showing the class data.

Lesson 18

Our holidays

- This is where Class 1 went on holiday.
- Look at the block graph, then read the questions.

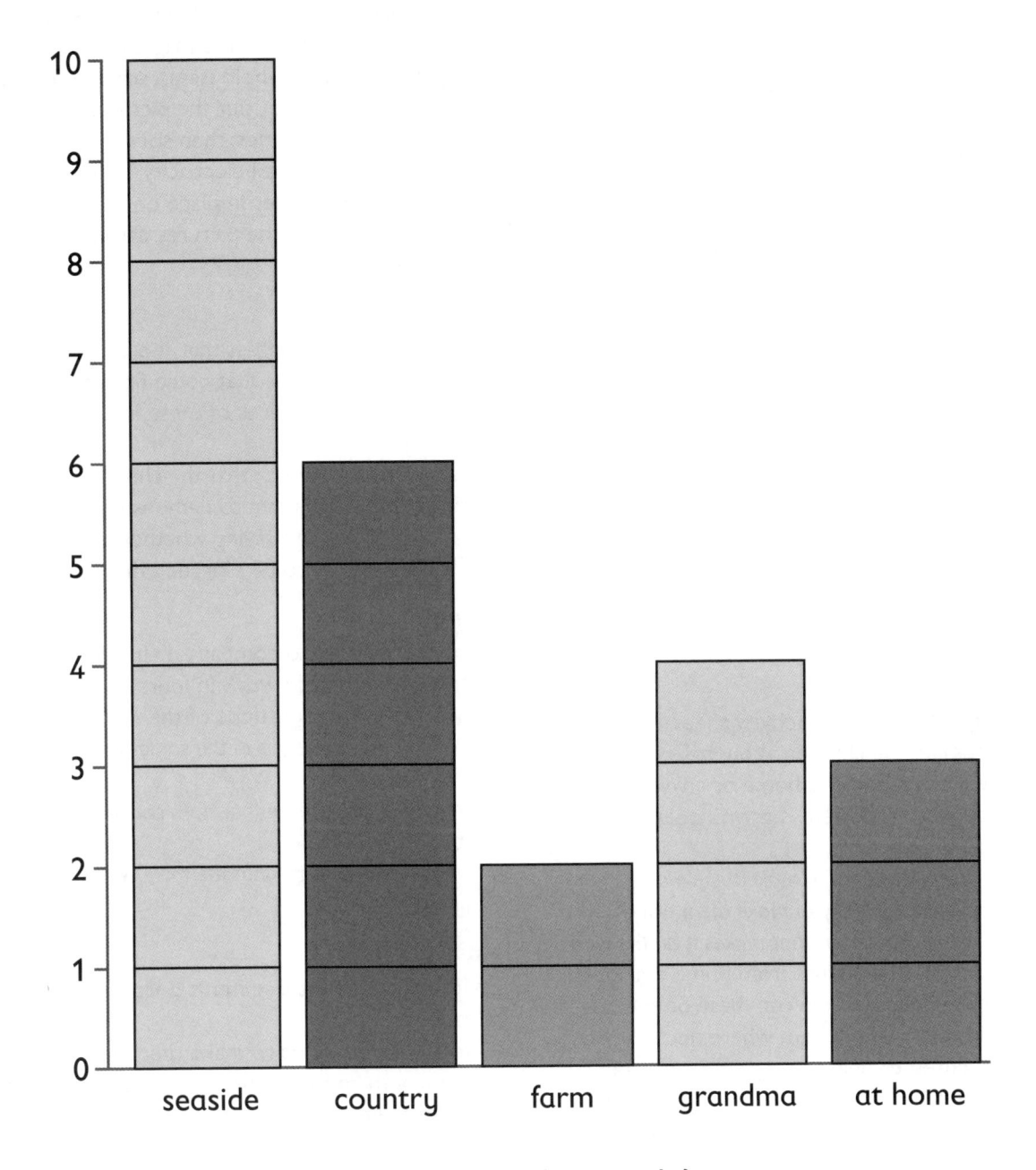

1. How many children went on holiday to the seaside?
2. How many fewer went to the country?
3. How many stayed at home, or went to Grandma's, altogether?
4. How many more went to the country than stayed at Grandma's?
5. How many children are there altogether?

Things that work with electricity

Lesson 19

Mathematics learning objectives
Framework:
- **U&A**: Answer a question by selecting and using suitable equipment, and sorting information, shapes or objects; display results using tables and pictures.
- **U&A**: Describe ways of solving puzzles and problems, explaining choices and decisions orally or using pictures.
- **HD**: Answer a question by recording information in lists and tables; present outcomes using practical resources, pictures, block graphs or pictograms.

NC: Ma2, 1a-c; Ma2, 1g; Ma2, 5a-b

Science learning objective
- **Sc4, 1a**: About everyday appliances that use electricity.

Vocabulary
Group, pictogram, sort, table

Resources
- Magazines or catalogues with pictures of household items, safety scissors and glue sticks

CD-ROM slideshow:
- Activity sheets: 'Electricity in the home' (also p43), and 'Electricity' (one A3 copy for each child)
- Image: 'Hi-tech equipment'

Introduction
Display the simple table on the activity sheet 'Electricity in the home'. Remind the children about safety when working with electrical items at home or anywhere else. Ask them to say what each item is as you point to it and then ask questions such as:
- *Which items need electricity to make them work?*
- *Which do not need electricity to make them work?*
- *How do you use a spoon? So what makes it do the work?*

Invite suggestions of other things from home that need electricity to make them work. Write these on the board, drawing a quick sketch of the item where necessary. Then ask the children to help to suggest things from home that do not need electricity to work and make a list, again with brief sketches as necessary. Discuss the questions on the activity sheet. Then ask the following questions, pointing to specific items in the lists:
- *How does this work, and what does it do?*
- *Which things in the list use electricity/use rechargeable batteries?*

Children's task
Provide each child with an A3 copy of the activity sheet 'Electricity'. Also provide the magazines or catalogues with pictures of household items, scissors and glue. Ask the children to cut out the pictures of household items from the magazines, then sort them according to whether the items need electricity to work or not. They should glue the pictures in place on the table. Remind the children to place the pictures carefully so that their two columns line up.

Differentiation
More confident: Suggest that the children think of other household items that could fit onto the table. They could draw pictures of these in the appropriate columns.

Less confident: Check that the children understand the sorting criteria. Ask them to demonstrate this by choosing different pictures and saying whether or not the item needs batteries or to be plugged into mains electricity.

Review
Invite the children to compare their table with a partner's and then to work in fours to make the comparisons. Ask questions of the whole class such as:
- *Did you sort the items in the same way?*
- *What was different? Why?*
- *What did you choose that does not need electricity to make it work?*
- *What else could go onto the table? Where would you place it?*

Now try this...
Children can draw these items onto a simple pictogram or table:
- toys (use batteries to make them work or not)
- classroom and school-office items (use electricity to make them work or not).

CD-ROM follow-up material
Reveal the image 'Hi-tech equipment' from the CD-ROM. Ask the children to identify which items need batteries and which need electricity. Encourage discussion about this as, for example, some cameras use rechargeable batteries, while others use batteries that are disposable.

Lesson 19

Electricity in the home

■ This table shows some items found in the home that use electricity and some that do not.
■ Look at the table, then read the questions below.

Uses electricity	Does not use electricity
television	spoon
microwave	bed
telephone	magazine
computer	chair
lamp	table

1. What things in your bedroom use electricity to make them work?
2. What things in your bedroom do not use electricity?
3. What else can you think of from home that uses electricity?

Scholastic Data Handling Year 1

PHOTOCOPIABLE
www.scholastic.co.uk

Farm animals

Lesson 20

Mathematics learning objectives
Framework:
- **U&A:** Describe ways of solving puzzles and problems, explaining choices and decisions orally or using pictures.
- **HD:** Use diagrams to sort objects into groups according to a given criterion; suggest a different criterion for grouping the same objects.

NC: Ma2, 1g; Ma2, 5a-b

Science learning objective (NC)
- **Sc2, 4b:** Group living things according to observable similarities and differences.

Vocabulary
Group, pictogram, set, sort

Resources
- Sets of farm animals – either models or small animal templates, safety scissors and glue sticks

CD-ROM slideshow:
- Activity sheets: 'Farm animals' and 'Farm animals pictogram' (both enlarged to A3), and 'At the zoo' (also p45)
- Images: 'Elephant', 'Giraffe and zebra', 'Seahorses', 'Ducks', 'Monkey' and 'Kangaroo'

Introduction
Show children the 'Farm animals' activity sheet, or use the models. Ask the children to tell you something about each farm animal. Focus on their similarities and differences. Discuss why you would find each animal on a farm. Ask, for example:
- *What does this animal give us?*
- *How do we use this animal?*
- *Do we use any of these animals in more than one way?*
- *Can you see any similarities between all/some of the animals?*
- *What differences do you notice?*
- *How could we sort these animals?*

Children's task
This is an open activity to encourage the children to think about selecting their own criteria for sorting. Provide copies of the activity sheets 'Farm animals' and 'Farm animals pictogram'. Ask the children to quickly and carefully cut out the pictures, and to sort the animals by their chosen criterion. Next they should sort again, but by a different criterion. They then choose their preferred sorting method and glue the pictures in place onto the pictogram. Ask the children to write their own labels at the bottom of the columns.

Differentiation
More confident: Challenge the children to find more complicated sorting criteria. (Sorting by number of legs produces three sets.)

Less confident: Encourage the children to think about how they are going to sort and to explain this to you before they begin. Encourage them to find a different way, giving hints if necessary.

Review
Ask the children to compare their pictogram with a partner, then as a group of four. Then ask questions of the whole class such as:
- *How did you sort the animals?*
- *How many columns did you use on your pictogram?*
- *How else could you sort the animals?*
- *How is your way of sorting different from …'s?*

Choose one of the more complicated sorting methods, such as by number of legs, and ask, for example:
- *How many columns did this way of sorting need?*
- *Which column has the most/least animals?*
- *Why do you think that is?*
- *What other animal could go into the 'no legs' column?*

Display the activity sheet 'At the zoo'. Discuss the animals and the pictogram with the class and answer the questions. Ask each pair of children to think of another animal which could be added to each (or some, depending on ability) of the columns.

Now try this...
Children can sort pets by number of legs, size, colour. They can use pictures cut from magazines, or draw their own.

CD-ROM follow-up material
Display the animal images on the interactive whiteboard or on a computer which children can access. In pairs or threes, ask the children to group the animals according to similarities and differences. How many different groupings can they create? Some children should be able to create a pictogram.

Lesson 20

At the zoo

■ Answer the questions about this pictogram.

| no legs | 2 legs | 4 legs | 6 legs | 8 legs |

1. How were these animals sorted?
2. Name two more animals you would find at the zoo.
3. How many legs does each one have?
4. Where would they fit onto the pictogram?
5. What has more than eight legs?

Scholastic Data Handling Year 1

Model testing

Lesson 21

Mathematics learning objective
Framework:
- **HD:** Answer a question by recording information in lists and tables; present outcomes using practical resources, pictures, block graphs or pictograms.

NC: Ma2, 5a-b

Design and technology learning objectives (NC)
- **2d:** Assemble, join and combine materials and components.
- **4b:** Understand how mechanisms can be used in different ways (for example, wheels and axles, joints that allow movement).

Vocabulary
Block graph, list, table

Resources
- Construction kits, ramps for testing models; uniform non-standard units of length, such as cubes, rods, lengths of paper; metre sticks

CD-ROM slideshow:
- Activity sheets: 'Model testing', 'Model testing block graph' and 'Tests from Class 1B' (also p47)
- Block graph tool

Introduction
This activity is likely to take more than one lesson. The designing and making of the model could be one lesson, then the testing and recording of the data another.

Explain to the children that they will be making and testing models that will need to be able to be moved, and that you will be looking to see how far the model will run off a ramp. Show them the construction kits and ask questions such as:
- What will help your model to move further?
- How shall we measure how far the model has moved?

Agree that the measuring of distance will be from the bottom of the ramp, not the top, to simplify the measuring task. Explain that there is a range of units that can be used for the measuring task. The children should decide, in their groups, on which unit would be most suitable.

Children's task
Ask the children to work in groups of eight, and to pair off within their group. Each pair makes their model from a construction kit. Using a ramp they should test their models to make sure that they run, and decide on their unit of measure. The children record the distance the models run on the activity sheet 'Model testing'. Each model can have three tests. When all the testing is complete, the group uses the best test result from each pair's table and compiles a group block graph using the activity sheet 'Model testing block graph' or the block graph tool in the Kids Zone on the CD-ROM.

Differentiation
More confident: Ask the children to measure distances using centimetres.
Less confident: The children may need help with making sensible choices of units and measuring.

Review
Display the activity sheet 'Tests from Class 1B' and discuss the questions with the class. Ask the children to compare these results with their own.

Ask the children which model went furthest in each group. Discuss which units were chosen for measuring and how sensible the children thought their choices were. Reveal the block graph tool from the slideshow. Choose one group's graph and input the data into the tool as the children watch you do this. Ask questions such as:
- Which units were used?
- Do you think that this was a good choice? Why do you think that?
- Which model went furthest?
- How much further did that model go than this one? (Pointing at another result on the block graph.)
- Which two models had a difference of ... units in their results?
- How did you work that out?
- What was the difference between the highest and lowest scores?
- Are these scores similar to the ones that your group had?
- Why do you think that was?

Now try this...
Throw quoits or beanbags. Measure the distances thrown with uniform non-standard units, or metre sticks. Record these on a table and then make a block graph of the results.

CD-ROM follow-up material
Use the block graph tool on the CD-ROM to create a graph of the results of the 'Now try this' activity.

Lesson 21

Tests from Class 1B

- The children in Class 1B measured how far their models went in centimetres.
- Look at their block graph, then answer the questions.

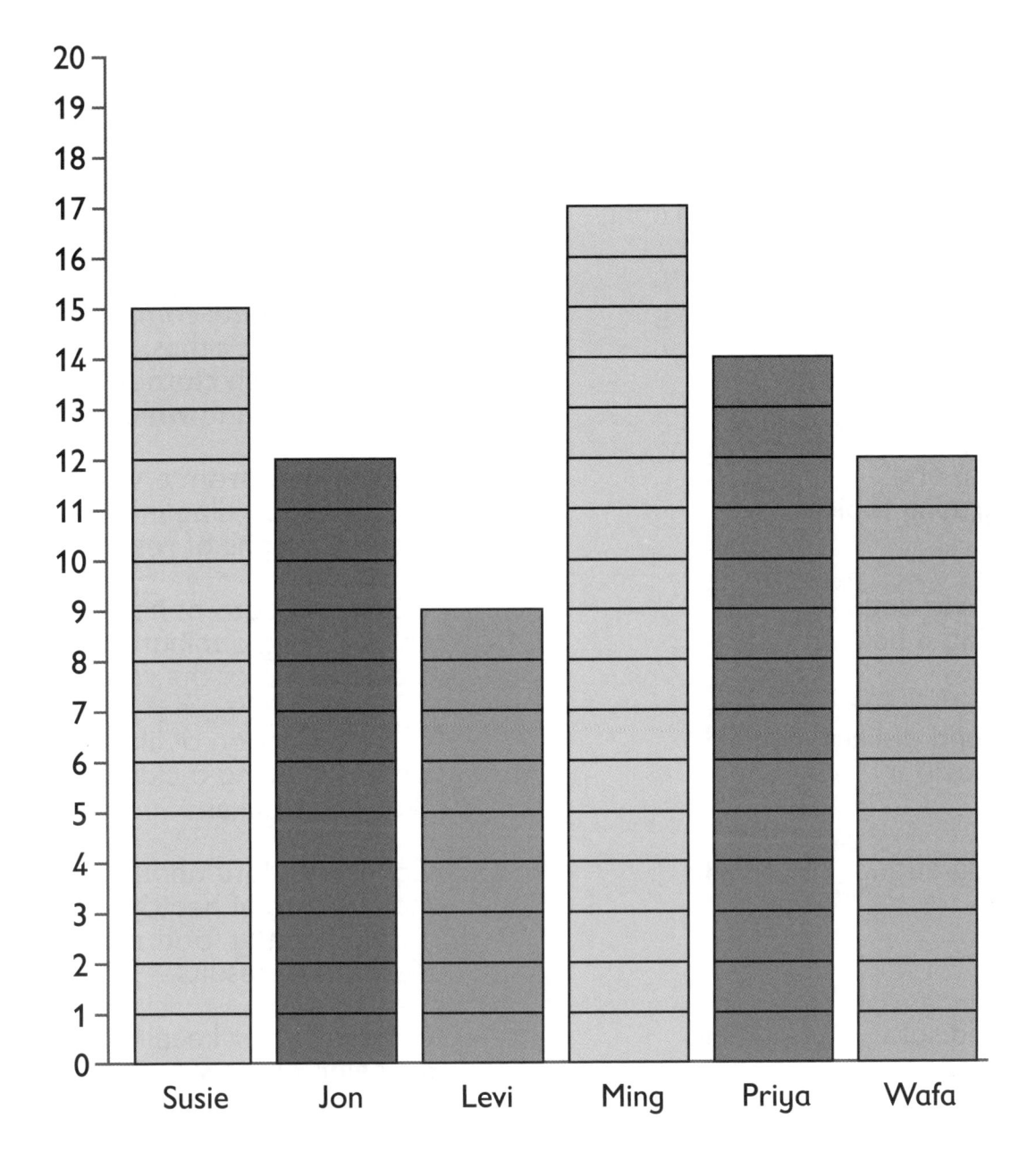

| | Susie | Jon | Levi | Ming | Priya | Wafa |

1. Whose model went furthest?
2. Which two models went the same distance?
3. What is the difference between Susie's result and Levi's?
4. How much further did Priya's model go than Jon's?
5. What is the difference between the least and the greatest distance?

Further ideas

Here are some further ideas for Handling Data across the curriculum.

Topic	Curriculum area	Handling data
How long does it take to travel to school?	Geography	Collecting data; recording results in a block graph
Information from a story	English	Collecting data. Recording results in a diagram or picture
Where were you born?	Geography	Collecting data; block graph to show results of birth place
Historical costumes, such as Victorian clothes	History	Collecting data; comparing with today's clothes; diagram to show which clothes are worn today, and which not
History and Geography topics	ICT	Finding data from a variety of sources; recording in tables; making graphs of results
Throwing and catching a ball	PE	Collecting data of how many times during a minute; making a class table of the results
Likes and dislikes of behaviour	PSHE	Class collection of likes and dislikes; making a class table of likes and dislikes
Healthy eating	PSHE	Collecting data about food; making lists of healthy and not so healthy food; making a diagram of results
Keeping safe	PSHE	Class rules for keeping safe; agreeing on how to record these so that they are easy to access
Sorting materials	Science	Sorting rock, paper, plastic, wood, etc by a criterion; sort again by another criterion; record each sorting in a simple diagram or picture